Edited by Don Briggs

BETWEEN YOU AND ME
First published November 1999 by

The Cottage Home
Tivoli Road
Dun Laoghaire
Co Dublin

Copyright this collection © 1999 Don Briggs

ISBN 1 873748 09 4

British Library Cataloguing in Publication Data
A catalogue record for this book is available from the British Library

The publishers wish to thank the following for their kind permission to
reproduce the following poems:
Michael B. Yeats for 'The Fiddler of Dooney' by W.B. Yeats
Beyond Words Publishing for 'There's a Hole in My Sidewalk' by Portia
Nelson copyright © Portia Nelson 1993

Cover design: Slick Fish Design
Cover Paintings: Louise Mansfield
'Summer Days' (front cover)
'Sandycove Days' (back cover)
Inside line drawings by Claire Maguire
Printed in Ireland by Colour Books Ltd.

BETWEEN YOU AND ME

Glimpses of Irish Childhood

Edited by Don Briggs

THE
COTTAGE
HOME FOR
LITTLE
CHILDREN

FOUNDED 1879

Contents

Acknowledgments

Where should I begin?

Well, the book couldn't have happened without the various authors, obviously, and they are due a huge debt of gratitude for their literary contributions and allowing the readers, in numerous cases, to enter the private world of their early upbringing. We are also grateful to those other authors and publishers who allowed us to reprint poems and quotations.

A number of people in the trade deserve a special mention for their active direction and advice. Special among these are Edwin Higel and Ciara Considine of New Island Books who gave seemingly endless hours of input to the project and to John Davey of Book Stop who provided very welcome sponsorship and also explained how the business worked. We are grateful for the willingness of Colour Books of Baldoyle to guide us through the print process as cost effectively as possible and to Nortons and Slick Fish Design for absorbing a portion of the design and artwork costs of the front and back covers. They had the pleasure of working with a pair of delightful oil paintings, kindly offered by Louise Mansfield.

While the short time span between project lift-off and finished product worked against our ambition to find a major sponsor, we did receive some financial support towards our production costs near publication date. While Book Stop and Batchelors Foods were particularly helpful in this regard, we are very grateful for all contributions, no matter how small, which will help to increase the percentage amount available for the charity.

A small team of committee members and friends of 'The Cottage Home' put a lot of work into bringing the book to print. While it would be their preference to remain anonymous, I believe it is only right to single out Alison Bernstein and our Secretary, Marilyn Lesh, for special mention. I also must thank Marguerite, my long suffering wife, for her active assistance throughout the project.

Finally, I thank you, the readers, for buying this book and thus supporting 'The Cottage Home'. Your patronage will allow us to provide 'our' children with a little more of the kind of comforts that most of us, as children, were able to enjoy in our own homes.

The Editor.

Preface

The Cottage Home is delighted with the response from so many people to the idea of compiling this book. Throughout its one hundred and twenty year history the home has depended on the assistance given by its friends and supporters to ensure that the quality of care which the home can offer can continue at a high standard. Help has come in many ways over these years and it is remarkable how new ways of providing support continue to be developed with great enthusiasm and imagination.

From its modest beginnings in 1879 as a crèche, or day nursery, the home soon became involved with residential care and in 1887 moved to its own purpose-built premises in Tivoli Road. Within a short time there were between forty and fifty children living in the Home, all under five years of age, in addition to those attending the day nursery. This number of residents continued to increase over many years and for a time early in the 20th century the Home had children up to seven or eight years of age before dropping back to a maximum of five years. As time went on and circumstances changed the number accommodated was reduced to twenty so that each child had more space and could be given more individual attention.

In more recent years the Cottage Home has acquired satellite houses and these are used for older children as the home now has children up to their mid-teens. A house was acquired close by in Myrtle Park for older boys and another in St. Joseph's Terrace, Tivoli Road for the girls, the latter now replaced by a larger and better-suited house in Ballinteer. The number of resident children remains at about twenty, though the spread into two other houses has improved the space available to each child. Day care continues in the main building where the younger residents live in rooms that have been subdivided from the original dormitories to give them a more domestic scale of bedroom.

The provision of good quality accommodation for the children who live in the home is a fundamental part of the Cottage Home's work, but it is not enough on its own. It is the additional facilities that the Home provides which add that extra facet to a child's time in the home. These include every day facilities such as an adventure playground, a gymnasium and cars for transporting children wherever they need to go. There is also a mobile home in Wicklow where the children can be brought for holidays during the summer, or even just weekend breaks. It is these extras which can only be provided through the special help which the Home receives from its friends and benefactors. This is also the source of the occasional more spectacular help such as the trip to Disneyland which some of the children enjoyed, not to mention various visits to other places, far and near, over the years.

Browsing through the history of the Cottage Home which was written for the centenary in 1979 by Olive C. Goodbody, we can see that the generosity in time and effort is no new phenomenon. The larger benefactions included the original designs of the home, the architect W. Kaye Parry being one of the committee members, and the cost of completing the east wing of the building which was borne by the widow of Thomas P. Cairnes, another committee member. Such gifts from individuals may be beyond the reach of most people, but the smaller contributions have also added up to a great deal over time.

The book also tells the story of one major incident that, while it revolves around the failure of a project, nevertheless showed how assistance from individuals and companies dovetailed so well. During the Second World War the government became concerned that the Home could be in danger should there be an attack on Dun Laoghaire and asked that the children be evacuated. The matron managed to arrange for a house in Ardee to be lent for the purpose and, with great support from staff who moved with the children, the evacuation was effected. Great kindness was shown by many people, both from Dun Laoghaire and Louth, who volunteered to visit the relocated home. However, the venture ended after less than a week when the water supply from the well dried up and a gang of volunteers, with the aid of two buses kindly lent by CIE, had the children fed and tucked up in their beds in Tivoli Road by 10 p.m.!

This tradition of support continues, as can be seen in the great deal of time and thought given freely by the various authors to fill the pages of this book. The trustees and committee of the home cannot thank all concerned enough for this demonstration of kindness. Space does not permit me to single out all of the contributors individually to thank them, but I would ask that when you look at the contents list you might spare a moment to reflect on the time and care which has gone into each piece and to thank the authors telepathically!

Rob Goodbody
Chairman, Cottage Home.

Introduction

As a very recent addition to the Committee of The Cottage Home, I am suitably impressed by the enormous amount it has managed to achieve without me for most of its one hundred and twenty years of existence.

Anybody involved in childcare today, even in the smallest way like me, is acutely conscious of the changing demands and expectations of young people, the difficulties of providing a modern, caring and yet safe environment to those children whose safety is at risk and the recent and most welcome fundamental questioning of the quality, safety and suitability of childcare facilities and services in our country.

Independent, voluntary or private homes are, in the main, still hugely dependent upon the State for the majority of their funding. While grant-support of the private homes is substantial and mainly unquestioning there tends to be a serious shortfall in the funds necessary to offer children a variety and quality of life they might expect in normal suburban homes. This is the shortfall that organisations like 'The Cottage Home' strive to cover through fund-raising activities such as this one.

When we set out on this project we had little idea as to the level of enthusiastic response we would receive from those lobbied to participate. I had been favourably impressed, on a number of occasions, by the way in which Ireland reacts so positively to the support of a good cause. My major ambition was to encourage a collection of pieces which were not just original but also brought the authors back to a time when they had little idea where their life was leading, making them just as normal as all the rest of us. The honesty and personal insight of the contributions is one of the key fascinations of this publication. I also believe the reader will share a tangible sense of the almost unexpected nostalgia and indeed fun which the authors experienced in collating their early experiences. I wanted to be in the slightly unusual position of asking for non-financial support for a charitable organisation from people who I imagine are a permanent target for funds for every good cause which the Irish support.... and the Irish do support every good cause.

The book, thankfully, largely produced itself and I made a conscious decision to avoid making more than minor changes to the submissions as that would have taken away from the authenticity of the whole exercise. One of the biggest dilemmas has been how to present the authors, particularly as a large number of them require no introduction. I hope that the decision to keep the titles as simple as possible will be acceptable to all parties.

Childhood memories are special for all of us. Though they may not always be positive or even necessarily pleasant they are highly evocative, sometimes embarrassing, often personal, always individual. I am very grateful to almost seventy contributors who were prepared to share their recollections with us and, in doing so, to allow us to invade their privacy.

As a total novice in the area of book editing, publishing and distribution, it was a great comfort to be surrounded by so much support from those with expertise in the subject. While this greatly reduced the load, there was still a lot of work involved and I have enjoyed it all so much that I definitely want to do it all again!

A number of the items included in this book were sent to us with introductory letters and personal notes which were interesting in their own right. I have chosen to print one of them here as I feel it epitomises the initial response of most people to the challenge of penning a memory and how capably they succeeded. This letter came from **John de Courcy Ireland**, a Maritime Historian, scholar and writer of many summers:

'Though I shall shortly with normal luck be eighty-eight, I seem to get busier with every month, one book just finished, publisher demanding the next, regular articles for a maritime 'historical' review and broadcasts for a maritime programme to organise, books to review, closing speech of an international conference to deliver yesterday - all my acquaintances seem sure I shan't stray far into new century and demand activities while I'm still around in this one!

Nevertheless, I was much touched by your appeal and was puzzling and puzzling what to do when I saw the child on Killiney beach whom I celebrated at 2 a.m. this morning in poor verse.

Probably this contribution is not what you want. If so don't hesitate to send it back — I should certainly not be offended and another sleepless night might inspire something better.

Very good luck with your inspired venture.

Small Child Seen By The Sea In Killiney Bay

Little child, your face all smiles
As the spent waves of the sea
Come to tickle your tiny feet
I think of the countless miles
The voyage of your life will be,
All its moments of cold and heat.'

These few lines have inspired some childhood memories of my own — how times have changed!

No central heating, just ice upon the inside panes

No traffic problems, no need for parking meters or bus lanes

No coloured telly, but black and white was still a treat

No lunar landings, first earthly orbits were quite a feat

No fax or e-mail, a telegram was really quick

No chocolate ice creams, but sherbet dabs were great to lick
No pounds on offer, but rich with half a crown
No Rapid Transport, to take you into town
No indication, that life back then would now seem strange
No regrets, no real desire, those childhood days at all to
change.

The book provides as much variety in subject matter as in the range of backgrounds, professions and interests of the contributors and yet I know that every reader will identify with many of the memories included. I certainly did and I don't believe there is a lot of difference … 'Between you and me'.

Don Briggs

First Principles

Sweet innocence of childhood ways
No negative intrusion
Fresh hope and joy of early days
Clear message, no confusion

Joan Millar

A Thought for the Day

Children are the star on the horizon
They keep the world moving forward
Their path is an adventure which covers many goals.
Their future hinges on health and happiness.
Circumstance is pivotal which we strive to understand.

Dorothy Kilroy

Childhood Memories

Chocolate eggs at Eastertime
Haystacks like domes all soft in which to tumble,
Ice cream stuffed deep down in crispy cones,
Liquorice laces, peggy's leg and sherbet dips to suck,
Dandelions topped with puffballs to blow away
   and tell the time
Hot coal fires for toasting forks aglow,
Old Maid and Snap and Snakes and Ladders
Oft told stories when it's time for bed
Days on the beach with sand between one's toes.

Measles and mumps and chicken pox,
Exams to dread and make the heart beat faster,
Monkeys and lions and tigers in the Zoo,
Ogres and giants and fairies in the pantomime,
Running races, sack and egg and spoon,
Icing as white as snow on Christmas cakes,
Endless hours spent shelling peas for Mother
Snowballs that numbed the palms to point of pain.

Sharon Bacon

I wrote this prayer in third class (with a little help from my mum) as part of a peace project that we were doing. I would have been about eight years old at the time.

Prayer for Peace

Jesus hear us when we pray,
Stay with us by night and day,
Ever loving by our side,
Be our comfort and our guide.
Throughout the world, in every land,
Let every race join hand in hand,
Together may they worship thee,
Oh grant us peace and unity.

Please Sir

The discipline of teacher's rule
A mixture of respect and fear
Life's future platforms built in school
First steps in fashioning career

Arthur Nachstern

One of my earliest childhood recollections was my first day at school.

Paula (my nannie) dressed me in my navy sailor suit complete with hat (this was the traditional uniform of infant children prior to the Revolution). I was very proud and excited. Mama, Granpapa, Granmama, Marta, the maid and cook all came out to see me off, as Papa and I climbed into the carriage, and off we went.

On arrival at the school we went to look for my teacher. After they spoke, Papa said "Bye Bye Arte" and walked towards the door. That was when it hit me, I was being left alone, Papa wasn't staying. I started to scream and cry and nothing they said could stop me.

Eventually, Papa sat me on his knee and said "Arte, I will leave my walking stick with the silver head with you (he never went anywhere without it). This calmed me down and he left. All morning I looked at that stick, standing in the corner where he had left it.

4

At noon, Papa came to collect me, gave me a big kiss and picked up his walking stick and we went home.

Unfortunately only a couple of years were left of childhood, carefree and no fears. In 1917, all that changed, and the world was never the same.

John Davey

My First School

At the age of four I headed off to school for the first time. The school was Windsor School at the top of the old YMCA building in Marlborough Street, Cork. The year was 1953. Windsor was presided over by the benign but firm Miss Hoare, to me at the time an old lady and blind in one eye. The school occupied the whole of the top floor of the building, one huge room split in two by a screen. We wore a brown uniform with black pumps for indoor wear. We could never be too rowdy or jump about because apparently the top floor was not entirely safe! On my first day I sat beside Pamela Dale who cried for the whole time but would not move from my side. Miss Hoare suggested to my Mother that I should bring an umbrella on the following day, but I seem to remember that Pamela eventually cheered up. On my way home I said to my Mother that that had been a great party and could I go again.

The school day always began with a hymn around the piano, invariably 'Onward Christian Soldiers' or 'All Things Bright and Beautiful', there may have been others but I don't remember them. There must have been lessons, and there was certainly talks about the Leprosy Mission. There was also gym — lower down in the building — conducted by the redoubtable Joan Denise Moriarty — who later became very famous in dance circles in Cork. She was also responsible for my first and only performance at the Cork Feis, reciting poetry. I have a vague recollection of standing on a huge stage looking out at a sea of faces and probably forgetting my lines.

Cork at that time usually had severe flooding once or twice a year. One day as we came down to the main door to be collected, we discovered that Marlborough Street had been turned into a river with dustbins floating by! How we were rescued I don't remember. I have a vague recollection of a rowing boat but that just might be a figment of an excited four year old's imagination.

After a year or so at Windsor I went on to "Big School", Cork Grammar, where I was followed a year later by Miss Hoare. The authorities must have decided that the top floor really was unsafe because Windsor School had been closed down.

It surprises me that I have such memories and such a warm feeling about Windsor almost fifty years later, it was a good introduction to school.

Carol Porter / Eileen Good

New Term

It was the first day of a new term in the playgroup. The mothers had left. We spent some time learning the names of new children. Among them was Brandon and Alan. Brandon was large, fair and slow of speech. Alan was small, dark and wiry. I began to organise the first activity. I looked around, Brandon and Alan had disappeared. I rushed into the hall.

There they were, sitting close together in that draughty place.

"Come back into the playroom," I said in a tone of authority. "No," they said. "We're waiting for our mothers." I tried to persuade them, telling them about the games and the fun we'd have. "No, we're waiting for our mothers". I puckered up my face as if I was going to cry, which I felt like doing. With a sniff and a sob, I said to myself "What am I going to do now." Brandon stood up and with a smile of pity, took my hand and led me back into the playroom.

We had a happy morning.

Barbara Cluskey

This poem is a great reflection on me as a child!

Excuses, Excuses
By Joyce Armor

I couldn't do my homework,
I had asthma and was wheezing,
I had nosebleeds, measles, heat rash,
And some very painful sneezing,
And itchy skin with blisters –
Oh so blotchy red and ivy –
Malaria and toothaches,
And a patch of poison ivy,
Eight spider and hair loss,
And a broken leg with scabies,
Rocky Mountain spotted fever,
And a full blown case of rabies.
I suffered – it was awful –
But I am feeling better now.
Could I have done my homework?
No, I really don't see how.

Noel Willoughby

A Class Room Memory:
"Put Rags On The Rope"

At school we had a teacher, whom we nicknamed "Rags". He got the name, not from the way he dressed ---- in fact he was always very smartly turned out. We called him "Rags" because of the advice he was always giving us. Frequently he would tell us, "Put rags on the rope". On first hearing it, we wondered what he meant, and in explanation he'd point us to a story in the book of the Prophet Jeremiah (Chapter 38). This story tells how the Prophet was imprisoned in a cistern in the prison yard. At the bottom of the cistern was a thick layer of mire which Jeremiah sank down into. There he would have died if a Palace official called Ebed-melech had not come to the rescue. He told the King what had been done to Jeremiah and at the King's command he was ordered to pull the Prophet out, before he died. He got hold of a rope, and some old clothing and rags, and lowered them to Jeremiah in the cistern, advising him to put the rags under his armpits to protect himself from the ropes. All he needed to pull out Jeremiah was the rope, but it might have cut into his flesh. The rags were added to avoid hurting him.

Our teacher saw this old incident not only as a story, but also as a Parable of life. What matters is not only the doing of a job, but how it is done. Many of the things we do, are spoiled by the way we do them. A bit like the cow giving the bucket of milk and then kicking it over. We can do good —

but do it repulsively, be efficient — but be efficient ruthlessly, be professional — but uncaringly. There has to be sensitivity.

Looking back on the life of Jesus, the Evangelist St. John described it as a life full of Grace and Truth. As our old teacher would have said "Always and everywhere he put rags on the rope."

Wallace Ewart

A Lunchtime Dilemma

The process which our minds employ to reveal their vast and ever increasing store of accumulated knowledge and memories is assuredly complex. There are things we wish to recall but are unable to, there are memories which flash intermittently across our consciousness, and there are those constant recollections which we enjoy and which are forever with us. Those early days at primary school fall unequivocally into this category – recollections encased in a rosy haze of well-being and happy days.

It was a comfortable cocoon; there was a sense of constantly interacting with that trinity of home, school and play. They merged seamlessly into each other so that each became an important part of the other.

Play was about creating a different world and absorbing yourself to such an extent that it virtually became reality. So in turn, Roy Rodgers and Tom Mix strode the streets of our village, to be replaced, in due season, by Robin Hood and Dick Turpin. There were no written scripts and no rehearsals, yet each scene unfolded in natural sequence with everyone slotting realistically into their part.

The dominating area of play was sport, and you took on the mantel of the heroes of the day, a Stanley Matthews, a Peter Doherty, a Johnny Carey in the soccer world or a Dennis Compton or a Ray Lindwall at cricket. We became those players as we played out our fantasies on every conceivable type of stadium from farmers' fields, to waste ground, to the village streets which thankfully did not have today's volume of motor traffic.

The interaction between home, play and school was nowhere more obvious than our lunchtime ritual. School was about five hundred metres from home. Lunchtime was the half-hour period starting at 12.30 p.m. and that was when football was played in the school yard. Boys from surrounding farms did not go home for lunch and so were available immediately for football. My dilemma was to get home, have lunch, and get back to school in such a way as to maximise the amount of time available to play football.

The obvious approach to this situation of running fast and eating quickly didn't yield acceptably consistent results, so other solutions had to be explored.

Our Headmaster was very sympathetic to this plight but equally aware of the opportunities which it presented. A set of arithmetic questions were set out at 11.30 a.m. The challenge – you could go home for lunch as soon as you had correctly completed them, or at 12.30, whichever was the earlier. What an incentive to accuracy in arithmetic, to learn techniques of fast addition and multiplication (all of which skills remain to this day and which I trust more than large fingers pressing on the tiny keys of some modern and impossibly small electronic calculator).

And so the challenge was set: could I finish the set of questions, make no mistakes, get out of school, run five hundred metres on eight year old legs, eat properly and drink my compulsory glass of milk without improper haste, run the five hundred metres back to school and be there at 12.30 to enjoy the full thirty minutes of football?

The routine was hectic, it was a double challenge which required speed and stamina (athletically speaking), and it required speed and accuracy (arithmetically speaking) and it had that glorious reward of a full thirty minutes on the football playground.

Things did occasionally get in the way and one particular occasion stands out. As I was on my way back to school, a few minutes later than I had hoped, I ran on at a major road intersection and collided, very forcibly, with the local constabulary. I picked myself up, and, luckily unharmed, set off at the same speed as before towards the inevitable football playground. I looked back over my shoulder in response to the cry of 'you boy, what's your name' and saw, sitting in the middle of the road, still entangled with his official bicycle, the local policeman, hat awry and looking none too pleased. My response was I suppose predictable – I did two things. I replied 'I can't remember' in that Tom Sawyer type of innocent belief that that would keep me out of prison, and secondly I didn't slacken my pace one inch. I was, I recall, sufficiently nervous about the situation to slow down at that intersection on all future occasions. However, I will always recall the mental picture of our local constable, legs and bicycle in an improbable collage against an asphalt backcloth, a fist shaking and in a commanding, if somewhat irritable, voice demanding my immediate return to the scene of his discomfort.

Be that as it may, the outcomes of such a lunchtime ritual were beneficial and the interest which such escapades engendered in terms of arithmetic and later mathematics, and in physical exercise through team games, proved to me to be a valuable foundation for the various directions which my career has taken. Perhaps it is primarily because those experiences became such an important part of my development that such recollections jump so vividly to mind.

And even that early brush with the law served to confirm that unquestioned belief in their stern authority to the extent that the laws they encourage us to obey, generally speaking, still determine the boundaries of my behaviour. Or perhaps it is because I know that my plea that I couldn't remember my name would have a somewhat less sympathetic response today than it had in the softer climes of village life – those few years ago.

Clodagh Kean

Not Regretted

When I was young,
not so long ago,
my fondest memories was to school,
I would go.

Running and weaving along the way,
in the sunshine or rain, always to play
Hockey or tennis, music and sport
it never really mattered,
what was the sort.

But, then came the lessons what can one say,
they had to be finished whatever the day.
I tried to avoid them come what may
but I soon realised I would need them some day.

Those days are all gone now
although not regretted,
I hope the future will be as unfettered.

David Moynan

The Headmaster

Students, more than scholars, at a west Dublin boarding school, Eric and I had just finished the Leaving Certificate and slipped off into Dublin city. Just a night out to celebrate. No harm done. No one the wiser. As we stepped off the bus on our way back to school a very familiar car passed by — the headmaster's! Over the wall and into the dormitory we rushed. No sign of the headmaster. But in the morning, just a little nod from the head. A just-to-let-you-know-that-I-know nod!

Letting young fellows become responsible.

Marie Danaswamy

Strict Rules

I was an only child, and at times I felt lonely at home without brothers or sisters. This, I suppose, is why my parents sent me off to boarding School when I was only eleven.

This was very different, when I found myself with up to seventy girls, mostly older than I was. For the most part, I was surrounded by friends in the school, but rules were strict and parents were only allowed to visit once a month.

This was particularly hard when my twelfth birthday came. There were no cards or presents or even a telephone call. My closest friends wished me , 'Happy Birthday', but by the end of the day, I was feeling very sorry for myself.

As always, 'Prep' was followed by Night Prayers, and we filed in silence off to our dormitories, with no more talk between us allowed until morning, As I passed along the corridor a teacher beckoned me into a room at the side. 'This is for you,' she said, handing me the largest bar of Cadbury's Milk Chocolate I had ever seen, together with a little card.

I will never forget dancing off to bed, the most popular girl in the dormitory, with the one Birthday present that stands out in my memory more than any other.

Geoff Chadwick

A Bus Ran Over It!

I was quite cute when I was eleven. One Monday in November I was cycling home from school after rehearsing Gilbert and Sullivan's "Trial by Jury" in which I played the part of a bridesmaid. The route from Harcourt Street to Stillorgan took me along Morehampton Road which in those days had neither cycle lanes nor bus corridors. My school bag, though heavily laden, seemed firmly fixed to the back-carrier as I cast a casual glance through the gates of Park House School at the junction with Herbert Park. I reaffirmed my opinion that the winter uniform was less attractive than the checked summer gingham. As I re-addressed my gaze to the road ahead I swerved to avoid a pedestrian. The sudden change in direction induced a dislodging of the school bag which landed in the path of a Number 10 bus.

They say your whole life passes before your eyes as disaster strikes. I can remember in vivid detail the patriotic green of the Leyland bus, the vibration of the left front mudguard and the grooves in the left front tyre as it scored a direct hit on the bag. There was a sickening tear as the bag distorted and two seams split. As the bus progressed relentlessly the bag disappeared into the narrow gap between the two back wheels and emerged a churned mess. I noticed the entrails included my pencil case — a small biscuit tin that was a souvenir of a school trip to Jacob's biscuit factory opposite the Adelaide Hospital in Peter Street — both institutions now relocated in west Dublin suburbs.

No one knew how Mooner Johnson acquired his nickname. Baring one's buttocks in public was not yet fashionable and our strict but amiable maths teacher was an unlikely trend setter. The fly in his trousers must have been all of two feet long, ending at the waist somewhere near his armpits and I swear he could have fastened the top button with his teeth. I approached with trepidation, my algebra home work complete and correct but the exercise book a sad, tattered and muddy offering as a result of its encounter the previous day with the Number 10.

"What happened to this?" asked Mooner. "A bus ran over it sir!" I replied.

The impact of the algebra book on the side of my head caused its final disintegration and the torn pages fluttered amongst my colleagues in the front desk, who were by now unable to contain their amusement.

"If you're going to lie to me you might at least make it plausible. A bus ran over it indeed!"

Culture Club

Those magic books that parents read
That made imagination leap
And when we snuggled down in bed
We dreamt about them in our sleep

Margrit Cruickshank

Stories

So many of my memories of childhood are centred round stories: walking with Dad along country roads, distracted from whinging by tales of snakes and tigers from his days in the Far East; perching on the arm of his chair (yes, those were the days when each father had His Chair) listening to him read about Winnie the Pooh and Eeyore, or Heidi, or Mowgli and Sheer Khan; knitting the same red woollen mitten week after week at school, dropping stitches, unravelling the mistakes of the previous week, heaping dark, secret curses on our crafts teacher yet lost in the spell of the stories she read out loud; listening to Dick Barton, Special Agent (and later, the Goon Show), ears pressed to the big cabinet radio in the sitting room; reading about the Secret Seven and Famous Five and acting out their adventures in gangs with secret passwords, invisible writing and jerry-built hideouts in the woods.

There was art, too: the stunning colour and design (unheard of in post-war Scotland) of the fairy story books sent over with food parcels (chocolate! sugar! dried fruits!) by our Swiss grandparents; the tin boxes painted with geranium-bright Swiss chalets against white pointy mountains and a blue, blue sky which contained at least thirty Caran D'Arche colouring pencils in every conceivable shade (the envy of all our classmates); the small wooden suitcases (also from Switzerland) into which were packed brushes and tens of tubes of watercolour: burnt ochre, crimson lake, magenta, cobalt blue, my mother's encouragement of our own attempts at art and crafts; the puppet theatre, built by my brother, from the papier mache we made. I painted the scenery and wrote the plays, my first adventure into writing for the public, I suppose. (We charged the neighbours' kid 2d a performance and provided lemonade and biscuits!)

And, of course, there was the garden with shed roofs to climb onto, bamboo canes to make bows and arrows from, trees to hang upside down in; and the river (full of sticklebacks and tadpoles), the quarry and the woods. We had bikes to cycle to the seaside on, and sledges and skates in winter. Nobody seemed to worry about us as long as we turned up in time for meals.

The sun was perhaps not always shining (though in memory, it usually does) but we had a freedom which today's kids can only imagine — or read about in books.

Tom Mathews

Book Time

My abiding memories of childhood involve my parents reading to me very early on. My mother read me Tennyson and Coleridge for the sound as much as anything I suppose, but I could imagine the Ancient Mariner with the albatross around his neck and the strange mirror world of the Lady of Shallott and still can.

My father read me the Alice books which I still love and Kipling's Jungle Book. I think reading to children is a wonderful idea. It gave me a taste for books that I have never lost.

Stella Mew

Early Introductions to Verse or Worse

It was the weekend, one of those special weekends when my father would be home, and I, aged about six, with my brother of about twelve, eagerly awaited his return.

He was in the Army, and we grew up in our family-home, based in Dublin, where my mother cared for our Grandmother, who was bed-ridden, while Dad was posted to barracks in Cork, Athlone or the Curragh.

His arrival home always caused a stir. Often it was chocolates or Turkish Delight for my mother, but ***always*** comics for my brother and me. He retreated happily with 'Rover' and 'Champion' while I went off with 'Dandy' and 'Beano' (Later on I knew that I, too, would have time with 'Rover' and 'Champion' which would be abandoned, once read.)

Bed times were always special too, because that was when Dad would come up and tell us stories. Mine were about Brer Rabbit and Brer Fox, and the tales became more exciting and more embellished all the time. As soon as the story ended, I was tucked in, and the light went off, and Dad would cross the landing to my brother's room.

After a few moments, I would slide out of bed and creep over to the door, so that I could hear my brother's 'Dick Barton' story, always judging the exact point at which the story might end, so that I could flee back to bed before I was discovered!

Sadly, although time passes slowly when one is young, the time came when Dad had run out of inspiration, and he could not remember or make up another Brer Rabbit story or another episode of Dick Barton.

By this stage, Big Brother felt that he was outgrowing bed-time stories, so Dick Barton was allowed to fade out. Not so, as far as I was concerned, and so my weary father reached out, one night, for something to read to me, instead. What came to hand was Henry Wadsworth Longfellow's 'Collected Poems', and my first introduction to 'The Song of Hiawatha'.

I still remember the magic of the scenes conjured up and my first real introduction to the cadences of verse. Longfellow, Macauley, Kipling, Service and Shakespeare, all followed, and then, as I, too, outgrew the bedtime stories, my own choice of Palgrave's 'Golden Treasury' and the Anglo-Irish writers took over, to be followed by many other poets and authors.

Even today, however, all I have to do is to read again from one of these favourite authors, and I am transported back to happy childhood days and the bed-time story that was so important in my early life, and has led to an abiding love of poetry and literature.

Niall MacMonagle

Seedtime

'Of course I may be remembering it all wrong after, after — how many years?'
Elizabeth Bishop

On the day I was invited to contribute to your book my seven year old daughter came home from her school Sports Day carrying a beribboned bronze medal. She was delighted. Having been presented with a silver medal she explained how she had swapped it for bronze because she already had a gold and silver at home and she liked having all three colours. That, for me, is what's best about childhood; innocent, imaginative and non-competitive. And then we grow up.

Our childhoods are short. It is what Wordsworth calls our 'fair seedtime' and what happens later is often determined by what we knew and did as children. Mine was very ordinary. It was Killarney, County Kerry in the 1950s and when I think about it I value it all the more because it was ordinary. We used to spend summers sitting on the wall across the way from our house taking down the numbers of the cars. Now there's an occupation in an idle hour. Try telling a child to do that today. Or we spent hours playing ball against the gable end, or planning excursions — the word picnic would give the wrong impression — to the Deer Park, a mile up the road on the edge of town, or digging our underground hut or building a tree hut in the garden. Sunday afternoons were spent in Muckross Gardens or down at Ross Castle or best of all

Rossbeigh Beach. Not even mass tourism has succeeded in destroying the truly beautiful bit of Kerry I grew up in but we just took it as normal that 'Heaven lay about us in our infancy'.

School is a blur. But I liked it. Rain on the long windows or a beautiful bird's nest drawn by Sister Posenti or our being asked to pray for special intentions are what I remember. And Mrs. McNeill's sweet shop on New Street took all our pennies. That I remember vividly: flying saucers and marshmallow mice and penny pineapple bars.

We went to no art classes, no speech and drama classes, no music lessons. Nobody did them. I read. Killarney had a marvellous Librarian. She had to huddle over a two-bar electric heater in winter in her overcoat but never lost her enthusiasm or interest in books. During the summer afternoons I would often finish the book I had borrowed that morning. Kitty would always keep me the books she knew I loved to devour.

Birthday parties were simple, modest affairs and always in people's houses. I learnt to cycle at 6.30 a.m. in the morning (it must have rained in summers but I don't remember it) in the grounds of the Cathedral while waiting to serve at seven o'clock mass in Latin. My brothers and I went on terrific holidays, most memorable to Uncles and Aunts in Tivoli in Cork and in Dungarvan; watching the Innisfallen — the old, big, round, black-bottomed one — going down the Lee or the daily trips to the Cunnigar in Dungarvan Bay — to be alive was very Heaven.

During the summers we also went to see plays in Killarney's Town Hall: 'The Country Boy', 'Bell, Book and

Candle'. In the winter it was the musical society with 'The Desert Song'. I can still feel the magic of waiting on the other side of the plush red curtain, a ribbon of light visible at stage level and excited feet preparing for the show. I can still see the fairy-tale setting of 'The White Horse Inn' when the curtain opened sometime in the early '60s and a woman with a yellow duster in her hand began to sing. I would never see a curtain in a theatre now.

Adults were extraordinarily kind and if they were as busy as adults today they didn't seem so. But they looked older, more formal, than today's thirty/forty somethings. The men always wore suits and collars and ties; women were still corseted; and in costumes for formal occasions. No jeans and runners, no baseball caps. They didn't jog or wear Walkmans or talk into mobile phones.

It was a different time. We stood and waved when Princess Grace drove down High Street and waved at us. John F. Kennedy died. I remember that from 1963 and how people cried. And I ran home more than once because the world was going to end at 3 o'clock.

I don't revisit the past that often but it's there. Childhood sets you up for life but there's no knowing what will follow on.

Anne Schulman

Nought To Nineteen

Born in Manchester (at a date still to be decided) our family moved to Dublin when I was a year old. I was not consulted.

It was safe to walk to the local junior school when I was young but in our childish minds the terrors of two Dublin eccentrics, Mad Mary and Forty-Coats, made it a heart-stopping adventure. She ate children and he collected the ones she'd missed — you guessed it — they disappeared without trace into one of his forty coats.

I took to crime at a tender age. My friend (a hardened criminal, age five and a half) and I stole two apples from an orchard. They were huge and ripe, ready to fall off the tree anyhow. As we walked down the road rubbing the juicy spoils on our sleeves an angry farmer bellowed at us and threatened to call the police. From then on I 'went straight'.

Academia sank gracefully into the sunset. The highlight of those years was a Royal Academy art exam which incurred my teacher's wrath. The offending entry had been returned with a large 'F' and a sarcastic enquiry as to whether it was intended as a joke. The subject matter was a bride and her two bridesmaids, the unfortunate bride had lime green hair. It was then I realised for the first time the drawbacks of being colour blind. The drawing was resubmitted with an explanation. After some weeks the slightly wilted bride (probably pregnant by then) was returned to me bearing a B+.

Like my mother, I was an avid reader, I couldn't face the day without a book. I devoured school stories, the William books, children's classics and, dare I say it, Enid Blyton. I helped out in a private local library, contentedly licking an ice cream held in one hand and stamping the books with the other. Does this qualify me as a librarian?

My parents were concerned about the sorry state of my education and suggested I might like to go to a boarding school in England. The Chalet School books immediately sprang to mind. Would I like that? I'd *love* it I shrieked. It was arranged that I would stay with my mother's family, who lived near the school, for a week before term began.

At that time meat was still scarce in England. The school trunk was packed together with a string bag bulging with steaks, a huge piece of beef and some lamb chops.

The second I set foot on the plane, my future career was decided. Flying was for me. The journey was without incident for about fifteen minutes until the pilot announced we would be returning to Dublin. On our way for the second time the stewardess, who had finished her incredibly glamorous job of serving coffee, came to sit beside me. I plagued her with questions, including the reason for our aborted flight. Two Alsatian dogs which were being transported in the hold had broken loose and were ripping the luggage apart and causing havoc. We didn't discuss the string bag in the hold, along with my school trunk!

There was an instant rapport with the family but the school had all the charm of a Dickensian workhouse. So began eighteen months of abject misery. There were no midnight feasts and we didn't play lacrosse, we played cricket against the boys' school instead.

The Easter break was short and I travelled to Manchester to join my father and meet his family. I did my best to ruin his short holiday by crying at every opportunity. My father, whose heart was about as hard as a marshmallow, accepted that my homesickness was unbearable and three months later I returned to Dublin.

Alexandra College and *boys*. Mainly those at University College Dublin which was beautifully positioned for our convenience on the opposite side of the road. They were halcyon days. I made new friends, suffered the trauma of a broken heart approximately every fourth week. The sun always seemed to shine.

Foolishly I dropped Irish as a subject so was ineligible for the Intermediate Examination. At fifteen I considered myself educated.

What to do next? My love of art was far greater than my talent so a compromise was reached, I enrolled in an Academy of Fashion. For years scraps of paper covered with fashion sketches — totally outlandish and impractical — occupied my childish fantasy. This could be the answer to *real art*. Several months later, having sewn a piece of green material with beige thread, I accepted the fact that I was not going to join the exalted ranks of great couturiers and left the colour-gifted to their task. With hindsight, it would have been difficult to have chosen a more inappropriate career.

Secretarial college. A breeze. All those funny little squiggles that were shorthand. The neatness of typing appealed to my eye. Bookkeeping didn't cause my heart to go pitter-pat but it was something to be learnt if not enjoyed.

Our local youth club offered places at a summer school in England and without much enthusiasm I added my name to the list. I was not the only reluctant student there, David Schulman had been dragooned by his friends to attend. It was there that I received my first bouquet of flowers. Romantic? Not really, they were cauliflowers. A year later I walked up the aisle to marry him, carrying, I am happy to say, the real thing.

Bugs and Bigger

Days on the farm or climbing trees
Amazing creatures in the zoo
Life's fascinating birds and bees
And animals and insects too

Fred Hanna

The Farm

When I was very young and into the early teens I went to stay with family friends at Cabra House near Kells while my parents went on their holidays. A lovely farm house with great big trees in the front and a large walled yard at the back with stables, cowsheds, chickens and horses. Everything looked giant size when one was young and small — perhaps if I saw the farm to-day it would look so different.

We lived in Dublin so it was a great treat to go into the country. I looked forward to seeing the animals, feeding the chickens, helping to make butter and many other things in running the farm.

A large saucepan filled with potatoes would boil on the range and when cooked I helped to mash by hand all the potatoes, mix with bran and perhaps other grain. It took a

33

while to get used to the feeling of the potatoes squelching through my fingers — but the hens loved the mixture.

Having milked the cows, the milk was poured into a stainless steel separator, a funny looking machine with a couple of spouts. As the handle was turned cream came out of the spout and milk out of the other — nobody knew how it worked!

Some days we made butter in a wooden barrel on a stand which went round and round by turning a handle until the contents were solid. We lifted the butter out of the churn and with two pieces of wood made it into squares and kept it in the cool larder.

All the machines had to be washed carefully after use in water gathered from a well in the yard and boiled on the range as we had no electricity or running hot or cold water in those days.

I remember the family had a number of birds and animals stuffed and preserved in glass cases on the landing. Sometimes they frightened me as I went up the stairs to bed carrying a paraffin lamp with a vase glass shade, it would flicker as I walked and the light would catch the eyes of the owl or an animal, they would look so real and I would jump with fright. We would bring up jugs of water to put into a bowl in the bedroom to wash ourselves and the toilets were outside the house so we had to remember to go outside before climbing the stairs to bed.

My favourite day was once a week we went by pony and trap into 'town' to buy groceries, corn, perhaps oil for the lamps etc. I would help harness the pony and hitch up the trap and off we went the few miles into the shops. Many shops had a large archway into a courtyard where people could leave their pony and trap while they went shopping. I would be allowed to hold the reins on the return journey which made me feel grown-up, but I think the pony knew its way home and really did not need my help.

My holiday seemed to go very quickly and it was suddenly time for my parents to collect me to go back to Dublin. I would think of those great days and dream of the farm and long for my next visit to Cabra House.

Carol Porter And Eileen Good

Rookie

A storm blew up. The branches of the Cypress trees in front of the house were moving wildly in the wind. Towards evening when the storm abated I went out and found three baby rooks, under the trees, calling incessantly for food and their parents. I fed them bread and milk, they were ravenous. Then I put each in an old plastic container, and left them, hoping their parents would find them.

Next morning one baby had disappeared, one was dead and one sat at the door of his container, opening and shutting his beak. He had lost his voice with all his calling. I fed him and put him in the shed. He became very tame and would sit on my wrist to be fed and would run up one arm and down the other looking for more food. I called him Rookie.

One day I put him in a covered box and took him to the playgroup. The children could hear his claws scratching on the floor of the box "What's in there?" they asked. "Wait till story time" I said. The story was about Pat and Mary who went for a walk in the wood, found a baby rook, tamed him and called him Rookie. "Now I'll show you Rookie". Such excitement as Rookie sat on my wrist, looking for food. They all wanted to stroke him. First one child stroked him, he ran up my arm. Then he came down for another bite and the next child stroked him and so on, until everyone had a turn and Rookie was full.

It was a happy day and remembered for a long, long time.

Declan Budd

The Wild Hockey

My parents in the 1920s had American friends, Ted and Helen Geisal, whom they had met when students. They used to go on holiday together in France and in Ireland. Ted would amuse them by drawing funny animals on cards and menus. On one visit to Dublin he played 'field hockey' in our back garden and afterwards drew this Wild Hockey. Ted's first book "And to think that I saw it on Mulberry Street" was turned down by many publishers before it was published at last in 1937. Every Christmas Day excitement would increase until we opened the latest book sent from America with extra animals drawn by Ted on the inside page. He wrote many books, including "the King's Stilts", which is dedicated to my sisters, "The five hundred Hats of Bartholomew Cubbins", and "The Lorax", "Thidwick the Big-Hearted Moose", and "the Cat in the Hat".

Ted's real name was Theodore Seuss Geisal and he wrote under the name Dr. Seuss.

A Wild Hockey for
my good friend Declan

— Dr. Seuss

David Moynan

The Kittens

Living on a farm meant we were close to the earth. Animals were born. Later they went to market and some even died. But there was always compassion and kindness. One day as a seven year old I was in a neighbouring farmer's yard and overheard Atty talk about "too many cats and more kittens about the place"! Sensing an ominous threat in his words I gathered up two kittens and hurried home with them. "Too many cats in Attys, now there are two many cats here!" , scolded my mother. Yet the kittens were allowed to stay. Soon they were *our* cats just as much loved as the rest of the family and the animals.

Compassion and kindness are still needed today.

Derek Briggs

What's That Butterfly

I lived at Kilgobbin from the age of two, My parents spent much of my early childhood restoring the two-hundred-year-old house and making it into a comfortable family home. It is granite-built and looks onto the Three-Rock Mountain, likewise granite (a crystalline rock that formed in the earth's crust) — so there was nothing there to inspire a future palaeontologist! But I did leave a fossil footprint at our previous house, in Glenageary. I confess that I've no recollection of this formative experience — my father placed my feet in soft cement while he was laying a concrete path — nor do I know whether the evidence survives.

Kilgobbin House had its own personality, with thick walls, low ceilings, and interior doors constructed for a more diminutive generation. (Growing up involved learning to duck into every room, and to avoid straightening up too fast!). The floorboards creaked; small boys couldn't get out of bed and wander around without tipping off parent or baby sitter in the kitchen below. In winter the huge beech trees in the garden groaned as the wind tossed them on a stormy night. Snug under the bedclothes seemed the most secure place as the rain clattered on the sash-windows — even if I occasionally imagined the trees crashing onto the house! A little further away yet more beech woods, around Kilgobbin Castle, were home to a rookery, which provided a raucous chorus, morning and evening, in the spring.

Summer was a different story. I remember lying on the lawn, listening drowsily to the drone of insects invading mother's flower beds. My father employed his two small sons as pest control officers (the vegetables were at risk) — cabbage white butterflies had a bounty on their heads (a halfpenny I think), although other butterflies were left well alone. We tried nets, but soon found that tennis racquets make the best swats.

I still have a fascination with insects, particularly fossil ones (including the beautiful preserved examples that are trapped in amber). But while the hum of insects on a summer's day is very evocative of that childhood garden, they make one sound that I dread — the high pitched whine that announces the presence of a mosquito in the bedroom on a summer's night, just as I've dozed off to sleep. I'm allergic not only to the noise; I once gave a conference presentation with one eye open, the other closed — after being bitten on the eyelid during a sleepless night in San Diego.

My brother and I used the paths in the garden as a race track, staging our own Olympics with teams of imaginary athletes! We roamed further afield on foot and bicycle with a freedom denied most children now. Bones were a particular interest (a Cow skull was borne home to adorn the wall of the yard), and my first excavation was prompted by the erosion of bones out of the bank of the stream that runs beyond the bottom of the garden. It was no dinosaur (of course) — just some long dead bovine.

Peter Gatenby

The Donnybrook Fox

In recent years we hear of "urban foxes", of foxes coming into Dublin suburbs from the country at night to search for food, usually by raiding dustbins. They are sometimes seen by the headlights of a car bringing people back from a late night party in the early hours of the morning.

In the 1930s for a fox to be at liberty was a rarity. As children, our family was responsible for a fox on the loose in the Donnybrook area in those years. We had received the gift of a fox cub while on holiday in Wicklow, and we kept it in a hutch in the back garden of our house in Pembroke Park. It was greatly admired and flourished and grew up under our care and attention.

When we were away on holiday the fox was left in the care of our neighbours who let the fox out of the hutch on a trial basis expecting it to return. However it escaped, probably into Herbert Park as a base. In those days several people kept hens in their back gardens in the neighbourhood. These were soon killed and eaten by our fox. Complaints were made to the police at Donnybrook Garda station about "Gatenby's fox."

One evening I heard from my bedroom at the back of our house shots being fired at the fox. This was by an armed Garda who was guarding the house of a judge in Clyde Road, and who aimed at the fox running down Clyde Lane. I am sure he was glad of the diversion during a boring job. However, he missed and the fox happily survived and continued its enterprising life in the area.

The scandal of "Gatenby's Fox" grew and there was some hostility to the Gatenby family who it was suggested had released the fox on purpose as an experiment on a respectable neighbourhood. Others did not take it so seriously and it was jokingly suggested that the Bray Harriers be invited to conduct a hunt.

As the raids by the fox became increasingly embarrassing my father decided something drastic had to be done. So he obtained the poison strychnine and placed it in the corpse of a hen which had been killed by the fox. This was left in our neighbour's hen run. Subsequently the fox died of strychnine poisoning, an unpleasant death, and I remember looking sadly at his stiff red haired body. So ends the story of the wayward fox of Donnybrook.

Don Conroy

Ghost Of The Night

As twilight falls upon the ruin
A blackbird scolds departing light
While woodcock roding at the moon
And bats take flight
Those messengers of the night.

A meditative silence around me crept
A silence so intense -
Had the world stopped to rest?

Alone I waited
With excitement and care.
For beware the castle lore
Of the demons and the ghosts
That stalk the night once more.

From out of dwellings dark
Came a hissing and a snoring
Then a shriek! My heart did leap.
No ghost or shade I saw
On a silent winged flight
But a beautiful white bird of night
Who made his home
Where king or squire once did rest.

Tar Attraction

At times our parents were appalled
We thought we were just 'having fun'
Some sticky moments are recalled
Odd things that we should not have done

Edwin Higel

A Thing Of Beauty

I come from Kitterburg, Germany — somebody's got to, as
Bill Bryson would say.

That village had located itself near the foothills of the
Black Forest but was still within striking distance of the river
Rhine and its regular post-winter floods, a fact that did not
make for rich farmers. Kittersburg was very small by German
standards, and — during my childhood years at least — had
what I would now call plenty of 'Easter European charm'.
Many houses, and especially the old millhouse just outside the
village, still bore the pock marks of artillery fire where both
sides must have used it for target practice during the dying
days of the war that had ended ten years earlier. There was no
communal water supply, and most houses still featured
sandstone-clad wells in working order and old-fashioned
pumps that supplied the individual farms and households.

But there were signs that the Economic Miracle that everybody talked about might reach us too at last.

I must have been three or four years old when a mighty commotion lured me away from my sandpit; the local council had decided to give the village's main thoroughfare a more contemporary surface. Lorries with trailers full of gravel arrived, even a monstrously large steam roller. The most fascinating implement, however, was a tanker-like structure with a roaring furnace beneath it which liquidised the tar and made it ready for application to the old and potholed road surface. This process produced a shiny black layer, which the men would then cover with gravel, spread expertly in even arches with their gleaming shovels.

I must have spent an hour or two watching all this quietly — never far away from the centre of action when the man spraying the tar kindly offered to apply some of it to my bare feet. I readily accepted, the tar wasn't too hot really, and in no time my feet looked a lot more attractive than those patent leather shoes that other children showed off at First Communions and weddings, as my version fitted much more snugly in the first place. The entire road gang agreed to a man that this was indeed a thing of beauty, and as I couldn't wait to show it to my mother and grandmother, I set off on my short journey home.

Unfortunately, the fresh and sharp-edged gravel that now adorned the street forced me to use its untreated fringes, and soon the shiny glory of the newly acquired footwear disappeared in a cluster of straw, grass, dust and, I suspect, worse. When I arrived home looking like some bizarre bird with fluffy webbed feet my mother, unsurprisingly, wouldn't listen to my side of the story, or the compelling reasons I put forward for my course of action, and she had to spend a fortnight's supply of precious home-made butter to try and dissolve the awful mess that had changed my appearance so radically — while at the same time threatening unspeakable punishments if I ever, ever did that again.

I must have broken into tears but found myself secretly consoled when I noticed my Gran wiping away what I hope were tears of laughter as she turned away to go outside, leaving the two of us to it.

CLAIRE M

Ruairi Quinn T.D.

Noises And Smells

Nearly fifty years later I can still smell the rag soaked in petrol having been dipped into the tank of the family car. It was a hot summer's day and the surface of Moyne Road in Ranelagh where we lived had been melted by the sun. Our hands and knees were covered in sticky tar.

Our mother demanded that my father and Uncle Kevin, who lived with us then, should clean us up. My brothers, Conor and Loughlin, along with others on the road had been messing with this new play stuff. Its pungent smell of heat, hope and summer in stark contrast to the sharpness of the petroleum spirit and the near magic way in which it could dissolve and wash away the black sticky tar of the melting roadway.

My sense of smell and the memories of strong pungent odours are central parts of my earliest memories as a child. We moved house during the Christmas of my fifth year from Ranelagh to Sandymount. Changing home and school meant that I did not re-enter school itself until the Easter of 1952 — just after my sixth birthday. It had been spoken of and talked about by my parents and myself during those winter months. I still have memories, somewhat obscure, of discussions with my mother about the new school — the big school as we called it. A school unlike the small play school that I had attended across the street from us in Moyne Road. A school that I would be attending alone. My two older brothers would not be there until the following September.

The giant step into the world of real school or big school as distinct from the informal playschools which I had previously attended took place abruptly and immediately after Easter of 1953.

I can still clearly recall and could yet still draw an accurate diagram of the sequence of entrance halls and rooms that my father brought me through to place me into First Form in St. Michael's. We had arrived after the commencement of class and all was quiet. Nobody was about. You could hear sounds coming from various classrooms. Uncertainty greeted us as my father tapped quietly on a number of doors to establish the correct classroom. The failed attempts to find the correct room only served to increase my apprehension. As we waited, I was aware of the increasing uncertainty and did not want him to leave me.

But the correct door was eventually found, tapped upon and was opened very quickly. A brief conversation took place. I was accepted and ushered into a classroom full of young boys. I was assigned my place beside another boy at one of the old double desks. Forty six years later myself and my desk companion of that day remain friends. Tom Crowe was his name.

When I looked back my father was gone. But I was soon distracted with the activity of the class. I don't recall how I got home that day but I know I was not collected by my father. I doubt too that I walked home even though the school was only four hundred metres from my new home and I would soon become very familiar with that journey. In those days the traffic was very light and the safety of children was something that everybody took for granted. Very soon I was walking to and from school anyway.

My abiding memory of the day though is of noises and smells. The sound of Tim Crowe's sniffling nose. The smell of the Plasticine or 'Marla' as we called it, the smell of the disinfectant in the timber floors of the school. On reflection I could probably have been a good cook as well as an architect.

School was good to me and I enjoyed it. I was fortunate.

The Fast Lane

Transported back to times when we
In principal paid little heed
In travelling from A to B
To do so at the greatest speed

Rosemary Smith

Introduction to Motor Racing

At the ripe old age of eleven, my father who was in the motor business, decided that it was high time for his daughter to learn to drive. The car in which I was to embark on this venture was a very ancient Vauxhall and for me the main problem was that the steering wheel was about two feet in diameter and because in those days I was quite small, I could only see through this steering wheel and the dashboard. However, I eagerly got behind the wheel and having mastered the pedals which I could barely reach, I had my first lesson in this monster of a car in about fifteen minutes.

After that I was considered good enough to sally forth on to the main piece of track, known as a road, in Bettystown, Co. Meath. Having manoeuvred around sand, potholes and the odd donkey and cart, we entered the metropolis of Bettystown

Village which, in those days, consisted of the Village Hall, five thatched cottages and a corrugated iron Post Office. We entered the village at the high speed of 4 miles per hour, sending pigs, hens and children scattering.

My mother, who for the first time in her life had been remarkably quiet, suggested that I might use the footbrake as we charged rapidly over lumps and bumps. Hastily, in my excitement, having visions of myself being the first woman Grand Prix racing driver, I slammed my foot on what I thought was the brake, but was in fact the accelerator, and to my mother's consternation and wild shouts, we hit the corrugated iron Post Office at a mighty rate of knots. The resounding crash woke me up from my little daydream as we came to a grinding halt in the shop doorway. The owner of the Post Office and bystanders were very understanding, but all in all, I really think that eleven was a bit young to be a grand prix racing driver!

James McCormick

Trams

It was a sad day when trams disappeared from our streets. They were a very important part of my childhood. There were three routes that concerned me. They all began at Nelson's Pillar in O'Connell Street, the Number 6 went as far as Blackrock, the 7 as far as Dun Laoghaire, which older members of my family still called Kingston, and the 8 as far as Dalkey.

They ran on cobbled streets on sunken metal tracks and obtained their power from overhead electric cables. They were all double deckers and the earlier ones had open compartments at the front and back of the upper deck. These open compartments were very popular with us children as they allowed the possibility of throwing things, such as spit, on those who were alighting or getting on. Talking of spit reminds me that there were notices threatening a forty shilling fine for spitting. This was a public health measure designed to reduce the spread of tuberculosis.

The place where we got on, normally occupied by the conductor with his leather satchel of change and tickets, had on the floor a small raised disc, which when stood upon rang a bell which was a signal to the driver to proceed. It is not surprising that we aspired to tread on this device.

Fares were modest. At one time I was obliged to go to Blackrock Baths, now long defunct, for swimming lessons. The fare to Blackrock was one penny and I was equipped with two pence before I set off. If I chose to walk home to

Monkstown I could use the remaining penny to buy two halfpenny Savoy bars of chocolate. Alternatively I could get ten NKM toffees which were sold not by weight but by number.

The service was frequent and, as they swayed and clanked along their journey, the device which made contact with the electric wires produced occasional vivid sparks and sometimes came adrift bringing the chariot to a halt. Their acceleration was not remarkable and this was a great advantage if one was bicycling, especially against the wind. By tucking in behind the tram and bicycling hard to maintain early position one was sucked along in the slipstream of the pantechnicon. The only risk was not sudden braking but getting one's wheels caught in the sunken tracks; this had to be avoided by crossing the tracks at something approaching a right angle. The only other hazard was the bone shaking affect of the uneven cobbles.

When I was much older, after the war, a favourite activity was the Gresham dress dance on Saturday nights, admission ten and sixpence. It was possible, as none of us had access to a car, to go by tram to the Pillar in full rig and to return by the last tram which left at midnight.

Trams were friendly and efficient, they seldom broke down. They were constrained by their tracks and unlikely to do anything unexpected. They had brakes which were probably not very effective and the earlier models had a sort of cow catcher device at the front which could scoop up straying children or animals.

There was reason to mourn their departure. It is interesting that new proposals like the Luas are more like a reincarnation of the tram than an extension of the bus.

Wendy-Jane Catherwood

There Is a Label on My Satchel

Clickerty Clack, Clickerty Clack,
The noise of the wheels along the track,
The sound and rhythm that I know,
Brings back the memories from long ago.

How many stops? How many stops?
Counting, counting, one, two, three,
Is it this one or the next,
Which is the stop that's the one for me?

An adult now, as this was long ago,
But I recall the days clearly, that I used to go,
A small little school girl, alert but tense,
It was scary for me but I did have sense.

Off to the station we would go,
Uniform smart from head to toe,
It was a short trip, for my mother and me,
But it was alone on the train, that I would be.

My big brown satchel upon my back,
Securely in place with two thick straps,
A large address label, there was upon it,
In case I got lost, on my solo school trip.

Counting, counting, one, two, three,
Missing my stop would be foolish of me,
But I wouldn't get lost, no not me,
As the label on my back was for all to see.

A short journey perhaps and no big deal,
But for the big girl of five, it was all so real,
That on a train today, as into my seat I drop,
My subconscious mind will count every stop.

David Moynan

Fast Passing Time

There was no speed trap in Castledermot that day. I did not even see the guard and noticed nothing unusual in the town. Yet as soon as I got home from school I knew something was seriously wrong. My father's car was in the yard. He wanted a word with me. The sergeant had spoken to him. It was serious — I had been seen speeding down the street in Castledermot on my bicycle.

Caring rather than interfering.

Tom Lawlor

A Moment In Time

The early morning light reflected from the lattice of steel tracks at Connolly station. I stood watching the silhouette of a man working on top of a tender digging coal towards the bunker. The movements so familiar to me yet unexpected. My father invited from retirement to perform an old ritual of driving a steam train from Dublin to Maynooth. I lift my camera... Click. A figure emerges from the steam below the engine... Click.

The station is filled with enthusiasm. Children on fathers' shoulders, jackets decorated with badges, cameras, videos, tape recorders. I watch the engine reverse towards the platform. Children cover their ears... click, as the sound fills and the steam obscures. A figure drops down between the tender and carriages, click, to make the coupling. Faces framed in carriage windows... Click. The vacuum break is created and the figure returns. The carriage doors slam in salute.

The organisers invited me to travel on the foot plate. I meet my father. He disguises his surprise with introductions. I stand in a corner and watch the ceremony. Green light ahead, whistle and green flag on the platform and his hand moves to a lever. The regulator is opened and the movement begins. The whistle is sounded and we cross over the lattice for the road to Maynooth, curving to the left, smoke and steam trailing. A sudden change of sound as we pass under a bridge. Canal on the left and the stands of Croke Park high to the right. The doors of the firebox are opened for the first feed of coal. I watch his hand adjust the reverser...click, shortening the stroke and making a new rhythm as we climb past Glasnevin junction leaving the city behind.

I'm watching my father controlling an old skill. Coaxing a piece of history across the dips, hollows and gradients, conserving steam for the journey ahead. Five generations of train-driving ending with him.

At Reilly's crossing the gates provide a vantage point for spectators. He blows the whistle and his hands make another adjustment, fine-tuning the speed... Click. He turns from the array of levers and dials. Taking some waste from his pockets he wipes his hands. Involuntarily I step towards him. My body remembering a homecoming ritual I wait for him to lift me. For a moment in time I became a child.

A Loving Spoonful

Doctor, doctor, please come quick
On you I am depending
I have a child that's feeling sick
But might just be pretending

David Lane

Prayer

"You can tell the Americans ... they look pasty and unhealthy, it's the central heating you know."

This quote from the 1930s was probably based on envy; certainly the cold at that time dominates my childhood memories. Ice on the inside of bedroom windows, snow lying for weeks and often chat of skating at the Zoo or on the Canal.

Certainly in matters of health the weather was very relevant. A chill or a drenching might be the prelude to various calamities. Pneumonia was often fatal, a "Strep throat" could lead to rheumatic fever with associated cardiac sequelae.

Infections of various sorts abounded. Tubercle bacilli could be inhaled with dust or swallowed in milk. A prick of a thorn might initiate infection leading to blood poisoning (septicaemia); indeed many doctors died from a needle prick during surgery.

Heat in various forms was used to try and control infections; commonly a poultice was suggested (bread, linseed oil and later Antiphlogistine) while in our household a popular torture consisted of H.B.F. (hot boracic fomentation); in this a piece of scalding lint was applied, for instance to a septic finger, in order to draw out the infection.

Small wonder that, faced with potentially lethal problems, most people resorted to Prayer!

But Penicillin and streptomycin and the like would change all that. Scientific advances could cure and recourse to the Almighty faded.

As a medical student in "Paddy Dun's" I witnessed the first case of osteomyelitis to be treated with Penicillin; for the senior clinicians a cure within a matter of days was little short of a miracle. Since then, over the past fifty years, there has been more scientific progress than occurred over millions of years.

On leaving school to train as a doctor my housemaster gave me a generous present of "Gray's Anatomy" inscribed as follows:

God and the doctor we both alike adore
but only when in trouble ... not before.
The trouble o'er both are alike requited,
God is forgotten and the doctor slighted.

Shane Ross

Life on the Ward

My most lasting memory as a child is the inside of a hospital. The year was 1956. I was six years old and suffering from TB of the spine. It was not a pleasant experience that lasted nearly a year, but when I look back on it, I feel quite cheerful. Cheerful because Ireland has come an awfully long way since.

Back in 1956 children were dying of TB. Medicine was not what it is today. The Health Service was pretty primitive.

Today we still rightly complain about health queues, lack of funding for hospitals and inequalities of treatment, but we live in a paradise compared with the grim fifties. I was one of the lucky ones. I survived. My parents were well off enough to be able to make me a private patient. I was placed in an enormous ward with dozens of public patients, all of them children.

The other children were allowed just one visiting time a week — Sunday afternoon. A rope was hung in a long line at the end of all the beds to prevent any physical contact between visiting parents and the children. Mince and tinned peas were the daily diet. The children and their distraught parents were made to feel grateful for the crumbs from the State's table.

I did not suffer the same fate as the others. I was allowed far more visits than they had. The dreaded rope was never there when my parents came. I was not forced to live on mince and tinned peas. I was grateful but acutely embarrassed. I told my fellow six-year-olds that I received better treatment because I was a Protestant!

At the end of six months, I was flown to London because my condition had worsened. Medical treatment was better in England in those days. An operation set me on the road to recovery.

Today as I look back on Ireland in the grim fifties I think it may be a time to be happy, not sad. Today Irish medicine is advanced. A sparkling new hospital has just been opened in Tallaght, Co. Dublin. People now demand medical treatment as a right. Few patients are forced to go overseas for a cure.

And today education in Ireland is second to none. The standard of free schools is better than that of fee-paying schools when I was a child. Young people of any background have a much greater chance of securing rewarding jobs.

Of course, terrible inequalities remain, especially in the area of healthcare. There are many minorities with special needs. But the children of the year 2000 can look forward to a happier future than the forgotten sick of the nineteen fifties.

Niall Webb

The Nursery

The memory that I will always carry of the Cottage Home is of going into the large Nursery which had a floor of mattresses. On the mattress could be twenty or thirty babies crawling all over each other, happy and content. The room would be full of baby gurgles and sounds. A most happy memory.

Wide Open Spaces

As children in our innocence
With no idea of scale or space
We thought we owned the world and hence
Our world became a special place

Julie Parsons

Going Back

Tell us about when you were a little girl.

This was the cry every evening when my mother came to put myself and my younger brother to bed. And what stories she had for us. Of living in a place called a 'rectory', next door to a church called The Mariners, in a town with a name that was pronounced Done Leery, but was spelt completely differently.

Of a world where night fell at four o'clock in the afternoon during the winter and in summer the sun shone till nearly midnight. Of a pier (whatever that was) where she and her father walked every morning, and listened to the band playing in the evening. Of gas lamps flickering and sound of horses' hooves on the street outside, as the cab waited to take her to board the Mail Boat for England. Of church four times on

Sunday, and lunch with all the family — grandparents, elderly uncles and aunts, cousins who played hide and seek and spin the bottle in rambling old houses where maids and cooks laboured below stairs.

So far away from the bright shiny world of New Zealand in the 1950s where she lived with us now. Myself, my sister and two brothers. Where Christmas was at midsummer, and the sand on the beach was so hot that it would burn the soles of your feet — even though we went everywhere barefoot and wore bathing suits from morning till bed time. Where the houses were made of wood, and could be shifted from site to site on an enormous flat bed truck. Where crickets sang after dark and the Southern Cross hung like a diamond brooch in the night sky.

And now at last we were going to see it all for ourselves. Because seven years after my father had been lost at sea, in the vastness of the south Pacific, we were going home.

At least that's what my mother called it. Home to Ireland, the place she had longed for all the seventeen years she had lived away from it. I said my goodbyes — to the green water of the creek which ran down to the sea. To the red flowers of the pohutakawa trees which hung over the cliffs. To the huge flat rocks where I had lazed and day dreamed and teased the fronded sea anemones in the pools. And I said goodbye to my childhood.

That was thirty-six years ago. And I still remember the chill of that May morning when we arrived in Dun Laoghaire. Six weeks by sea from Auckland to Southampton. Then overnight by train and boat to Ireland. It was grey and cold that day. My toes in my sandals, burnt brown from the trip, turned blue, as we waited and waited for our luggage to be unloaded. So this was our new home. How pale everyone looked, unhealthy, different. They say you can never go back. I looked at my mother's face. And wondered what she was thinking.

And now I too am about to go back. To New Zealand, to a writer's festival in October 1999. To search for the places of my childhood. And what will I find? My childhood self, I hope. Intact and happy. The way all childhoods should be.

Eithne Viney

Bundoran

When I started rummaging among my childhood memories some special ones popped up: those that were out of the ordinary; and it seemed a pity that everyday life in a lovely valley in west Cavan should recede into such a monochrome background.

We lived thirty miles from the sea and I saw it for the first time when we went on a holiday to Bundoran when I was about eight. That holiday started an obsession that still survives; a metaphysical relationship, laced with wonder and curiosity. I am never happy far away from the sea, and it has to be the wide Atlantic Ocean, because that was what I first saw. Others — the Irish Sea, the Mediterranean — are just stretches of water.

I still remember the smell of a rubber bathing cap, the breath-taking moment when a big wave plunged me into a maelstrom of water and foam, the taste of my first vanilla ice cream in the electrified metropolis of the seaside town. The lovely valley of my youth had a lot of things going for it, but it didn't have refrigerators — or the sea.

Sister Stanislaus Kennedy

Childhood Silences

Walking through fields
Up hillsides
In boglands
    Walking with sheep, cattle, horses
    and ponies
    Tending and caring
    and ducks.
Making, saving hay
Cutting, saving turf
Sowing and reaping
Making bread, churning butter
Milk cows
Feeding calves
    Roaming barefoot along streams and rivers
    Sitting on riverbanks
    Fishing for trout
    In silence.
Listening to the sounds
Naming their maker
Where they come from
Repeating the sounds
Remembering the sounds
And knowing
Why

In silence.

Gerard Buchanan

The Lamplighter

My first home was in the country, beyond Rathfarnham. The house was in the middle of a substantial farm and was surrounded by fields, woods and a river and was an ideal place for a child. Then the blow fell, my father was promoted and this meant that he had to move into the City. For a four year old this was not funny and I howled loudly and said I wanted to go home. In fact I howled every evening at bedtime saying that I wanted to go home. Then one autumn evening as the light was beginning to fade I was looking out the sitting room window and I saw a man with a bicycle and a long pole with a flame on the end of it, come up to the lamp-post on the pavement outside the house. He propped the bicycle against the post, bent down and opened a little door at the base of the post and put his hand inside and then he put the flame into the lamp which lit up. I was mesmerised, forgot to howl and it became a daily ritual at dusk to wait for the lamplighter and I settled down to a happy childhood in the City of Dublin.

Jennifer Johnston

H.A.P.P.Y.

Wet days and dry days, storms, heat waves, sun or great grey clouds in Greystones, all run together in my head, one long amorphous day, the only constant memory being the coldness of the sea; that was something you could never forget. Whether it was blue and sparkling or a dull heaving grey, it was always cold, no hint of Gulf Stream here on the East coast, no charming dips and flips for the faint hearted, this was bathing for fools or the children and grandchildren of steely hearted Victorians.

Every year for about two months we were deposited in my aunt's comfortable house. It ran like clockwork; in an orderly fashion the clock chimed our days away, rain or shine, we were ruled by time, or anyway we the children were; I think the grownups may have had more leeway, but we seldom saw them, so I don't really know. Beach time was from eleven o'clock to about a quarter to one, when like a flock of birds most human beings on the beach rose with a flapping of rugs and towels, wet bathing togs, the mews and cries of gathering flocks and migrated back to their houses for one o'clock lunch.

During the first two weeks of August an organisation called the C.S.S.M. held religious services on the beach. Just between the two arches under the railway line, shiny faced young men and women built a bank of sand which each day they would decorate with flowers and ferns and holy texts written in shells. "God is love," we would read one day; on another "Washed in the blood of the Lamb". Having a rather over-active imagination I found that text rather hard to take and spent quite a lot of time envisaging the young men and women stripping off their striped blazers and grappling with sheep in the field at the back of the railway.

Creepy! However I kept my thoughts to myself. In front of the bank we would dig bunkers and settle ourselves down for an hour's entertainment. Our nannies, relieved of responsibility for an hour would wheel the very young away in their prams to the Bonne Bouche where they would drink coffee and gossip, while we, Protestant and Catholic alike, were watched over by God and his shining foot soldiers.

Mainly we sang. There were short homilies and the odd prayer or two, but mainly we sang to the sound of a harmonium which was plonked beside the mound.

I am H.A.P.P.Y.
I am H.A.P.P.Y.
I know I am, I'm sure I am
I am H.A.P.P.Y.

In our little bunkers, we enjoyed such certainty, rain or shine, it never seemed to matter.

We were all definitely H.A.P.P.Y.

Perhaps none of us have ever been so happy again.

Mary Davies

Recapturing The Lost Spring

Until I was ten, I had an idyllic childhood. We lived in the country, a thousand feet above sea level, looking across a wide, enclosed valley to the heathery mountain beyond. The valley was a place of echoes and far-carrying sounds: distant children's voices, dogs barking, a farmer urging on his cattle.

Our garden on the hilltop was full of secret places to play away from the eyes of adults; I built whole villages of clay mud walls in the flower beds and sailed imaginary ships to distant continents along the waves of the gravel paths. Frogs appeared unexpectedly in damp, shady corners and on hot summer days elusive lizards sunned themselves on the dry-stone walls. We kept fowl and in spring there were broody hens to watch over and baby chicks to cosset by the stove.

It was a time of freedom. My friends and I played house in an old wrecked car down in the valley bottom, built dams in the streams, brought home tadpoles in spring from a quarry pool. In late summer we crossed the valley and gathered armfuls of purple heather, looking back from the opposite mountain at our scattered houses, strangely unfamiliar in the distance.

I remember the winters as uncomfortably cold, with lingering snow at that altitude, and the misery of chilblains and frozen pipes. But I remember best the spring, when there were fields full of cowslips and woods full of bluebells, and when the call of the cuckoo joined with the anxious bleating, near and far, of lambs and their mothers.

There was a particular quality of those sounds of spring echoing across the valley that haunted me into adulthood. For our family fortunes changed and we left the mountain to live in the centre of town. New friends, a new school, seaside holidays, a bicycle on which to explore new landscapes — I was not a deprived child. But I was always homesick for the country and the garden on the hill. It was only when, many years later, I eventually had a rural place of my own that the fierce nostalgia subsided — some faint ghost of it haunts me still. And it was only when I went back on a rare visit, by chance in spring, that I understood that there was indeed a unique quality to the echoing sounds in that particular valley. For there they still were, the urgent lambs and the noisy cuckoo, sounding clear through the spring air exactly as they had in my memory for over half a lifetime.

Michael Viney

Uncle Frank

Uncle Frank in Oxford was not entirely pleased to receive me as an evacuee, his sister's nine-year-old with this thing about flowers, so odd in a lad. "Sit down and finish your dinner!" Bleak as a Red Indian, when all I wanted to know was which piece of the garden I could sow my marigolds in.

There was no garden at home, just a mossy backyard at the middle of town, with dustbins and weeds. But some had flowers — pimpernel, speedwell, deadnettle — enough for posies in egg-cups. Later, sent up the hill with a pail, I brought my mother dandelion-heads from the graveyard, thick and golden around the white tombs. She made wine with them, for Christmas.

In the war there were empty houses and tangled gardens. I brought her blowsy tea-roses that spilled all over the floor, and once, a great white paeony for a vase all to itself. Later, when we moved to the edge of town, there were yellow Californian poppies on the dump at the top of the valley. And on the chalk cliffs at the bottom of the street grew wild sea-stocks, their clovery fragrance strong as bottled scent.

I climbed for them. I cycled out into the Weald in spring for primroses and bluebells, absurd, extravagant sheafs of bluebells sagging over the handlebars. Her name was Lily, but you wouldn't make too much of that.

Air Raid Warnings

There was a time not long ago
Right up above the clouds so high
When wartime children came to know
Of danger lurking in the sky

Feargal Quinn

The Field

I was six-and-a-half when we moved house in May 1943 to live in Clontarf. The main topic of adult conversation at the time was 'The War'. I knew that we were the 'good guys' who were not fighting and that it was important to tell any aeroplanes that arrived over Ireland just where they were.

My first memory of our home was the 'field'. It was covered in daisies and buttercups and I was immediately excited at the similarity between the colours of the field and our national flag, although I knew that gold of the buttercups was not quite the orange of the flag.

I set myself a challenge. I would save Ireland from any lost bomber whose pilot did not know where he was when he arrived over our shores. The challenge was to make the field into a flag by picking all the daisies and buttercups in one third of the field leaving only the green; by picking the buttercups in the next third leaving only white; by picking all the daisies in the last third leaving only the buttercups. The result was to be a huge Tricolour.

So each day I got up early and worked on my 'field flag' that was going to save Ireland.

I would love to claim I succeeded. The truth is the daisies and buttercups grew faster than my little hands could pick them. Before I knew it, summer had arrived and the buttercups disappeared.

But then again maybe I did succeed, who knows?

Don Tidey

Some Childhood

The Second World War started on the 4th of September 1939.
Within a very few days I became a very early evacuee, being
sent from London to the countryside forty miles to the south
and ten miles from the English Channel. For the next six years
a tiny part of that war was to pass me by in both directions. In
1940 it was fought overhead between Spitfires and Hurricanes
and German Messerschmidts. This was the famous Battle of
Britain — and I spent most of the time in the broom cupboard
under the stairs! Meanwhile, the German Dorniers and
Junkers 88 passed overhead on their way to bomb the capital,
two to three hundred planes a night. The day sky was filled
with anti-aircraft balloons, great silver bulbous shapes with
Mickey Mouse ears for fin-tails. The night sky was criss-
crossed with search light beams all probing for the elusive
aeroplane. When they found it, and they sometimes did, every
beam in the sky homed in and trapped it in a silvery glare, the
world around us erupted, and a veritable fireworks display
was produced by the gun emplacements around the village.

The nightly chore for a boy was to place specially made
wooden covers over all the windows of the house to prevent
any light escaping which could give enemy aircrews the slight
chance of pinpointing their position, or worse, dropping their
bombs! And, always the air-raid siren, wailing and wailing,
often several times a day, interrupting everybody's routines,
and especially school lessons. Sirens meant off to the musty
gloomy air-raid shelter again for a bottle of milk and a straw.

The sound all the grownups feared was the peal of church bells (which were silent during the war) and which would signal the imminent landing of German airborne troops, inland from the coast. The veterans of World War I, now left behind to become the Home Guard or Dad's Army, would have to take up arms and defend the country. It seemed to me most of them were so riddled with rheumatism from standing in the waterlogged trenches of France, that they could hardly walk let alone fight. The German paras never came, but by 1943 their Doodlebugs did. Nasty little cigar shaped rockets with a flame at the back and short rectangular wings all aimed at Greater London. Thankfully, many of them were pursued and it became a familiar sight to see a skilful spitfire pilot destabilising these weapons by tipping them over, using the Spitfire's wings, and send them crashing into the Sussex and Kent countryside.

Low level Messerschmidt raids were also coming across the Channel with random effects. One Sunday afternoon we were in the garden when we were strafed by Messerschmidts so low that we saw the eyes of the aircrew. They missed! Fifty years later, this incident was recalled pictorially in the local newspaper. I never dreamed it after all!

Now, you won't believe it, but one of the last hit and run sorties of the war happened in Brighton during a visit to my grandparents, and my father and I were once again caught in the street by German fighters spraying bullets all around us. They missed!! The evidence in the stonework is still there today, and also the sweet shop that I ran into and hid.

The tide was turning, in spite of the sinister V2 rocket (the forerunner of space exploration) which we could neither see nor hear, being aimed at London from Peenamunde. Every night there was the incessant drone overhead of hundreds of Blenheims, Halifaxes, and Wellingtons, as they made their laden way in the dark hours to Bremen, Stuttgart, Frankfurt, Cologne, Berlin and other German cities.

Dad's Army was now being reinforced by the Allies (funny word for a boy to understand). Suddenly the local park was commandeered by baseball playing Americans (not quite cricket). The big house was occupied by tough French Canadians, most shortly to die valiantly on the French coast in June. But then, I digress with all of this. I was asked to recall an interesting or amusing incident of my boyhood. Very difficult, I thought. Then, I remembered the French Canadians. As a ten year old boy, surrounded by war time influences, I was now old enough to be fascinated by these strange men and their ways. I peeled their potatoes, mounds and mounds of them, and watched and listened, and learned to chew gum. But, mostly, I recall that the French Canadians and indeed the Americans, had a particular way with the local ladies in the park and the surrounding fields, much to the dismay and apprehension of the remaining elderly population. The advantage these brave men had over the British Tommy passing through the locality was—nylons. Although I did not realise it then, in later years I can reflect that it was early evidence that — you'll get somewhere in life if you've got what (they'll) it takes. The brave French Canadians and Americans moved on to their destiny with D-Day and the Germans on June the 6th 1944.

I was to see these Canadians and Americans once more, two years later from a first floor window opposite the

Selfridges Clock in Oxford Street. The remaining few were numbered amongst the thousands of Allies whom I saw marching proudly in the Victory Parade on June the 9th 1946.

Howard Kilroy

Memories of a Wartime Baby

Upon being asked to write about my childhood with no writing skills I had to give a little thought to how I might approach the subject. After all, it was a long time ago. And being forced to look back is difficult for someone who has a "never look back" philosophy about life. I was forced to conclude also that this was going to be a rather uninteresting subject to others.

In thinking about childhood one is looking for a definition which in my case I consider to be my pre-teen years but there are, of course, those who would say I never grew up.

The overriding impression I would have of my childhood is one which came from a modest but very stable environment that started out based on old-fashioned family values. My father and mother, who are no longer around, are those to whom I owe everything. They made much sacrifice, but for them the pleasure was in the giving. They both came from country towns and came as a young and struggling couple to the big city with nothing but their dreams of a bright future.

My father was a counter hand, commercial traveller and then moved up to sales management. The commercial traveller part, which did at least provide a family car for the Sunday drives, meant an absent father for much of my life who made up for this loss of input through complete commitment on weekends to the family. Consequently, my mother had a huge influence on our lives in imparting value systems which last until this day. She was a great manager who made much of very little.

I was born in 1936 — a war-time baby in a sense — some of my earliest memories as a Northsider were of bombs falling on the North Strand, uncles who went to war returning in uniforms which provided for great romance and excitement, vegetable allotments growing needy food and father setting out with lorry loads of neighbours to cut turf for family heating when other fossil fuels were no longer available.

I came from a family of four—two brothers and a sister, all cunningly three years apart. We have always been close but as with all siblings, the occasional fight being the order of the day.

The influences in my young life were in no particular order of listing; school, church, scouting, sport, vacations and girls. Sadly no great record of those early days exist—this was before cine and video and there was clearly no culture of snapshots as there are no photographic records. I do have one great photograph of me walking with my father on O'Connell Street in my first new suit (short trousers, of course) and he used to tell me the story of meeting a friend who admired the suit and me brushing away a friendly hand indicating that the friend should not break it.

My home background was stern, somewhat disciplinary, but caring; though not an overtly touching and feeling scenario. My own character as it formed was not impressive. My intellect was modest and I was somewhat lazy, though competitive and fun loving. My parents loved music and I certainly failed them on that count abandoning piano lessons at early stage and my singing being reduced ultimately to bar room stuff. My mother in particular had such high hopes when at an early stage, singing duets with my brother, I used to win local hymn singing competitions.

School started at national school level. Howth Road School I remember as tough and I was not hugely receptive to teachers' efforts. Much time was spent at the back of the class and attending school would not have been a matter of joy. Physical punishment was the order of the day and that at least ensured a good grounding in basics. Because of economic circumstances it was important to get a scholarship to the next level and I eventually did get a second class entry to High School. My folks were pleased but I could have done better. Entering high school at twelve was an awesome experience but it did have a huge influence on my life despite being a mediocre student.

In saying church had an influence on my life it was not because of the religious implications but because of its social aspects—great place to meet people — even girls. And Sunday school outings are recalled with great joy. I was reared a Presbyterian even though Church of Ireland would have been more the family backdrop and that's the faith to which I returned. Sunday observance was a family standard and I recall many rows with my father about playing football on a Sunday.

Wolf Cubs and subsequently Scouting had a significant influence in many learning for life experiences. Self-sufficiency was learned through camping and outdoor activities also provided travel opportunities. My very first time outside of Ireland was through Scouting. The camaraderie was great. Physical development was also a part of scouting where cycling many miles with big backpacks was nothing extraordinary. And sports were an important part of scouting activity. My current involvement with Scouting is a recognition of payback time for the positive influences on my childhood.

Sport has always been important in my life and I suppose goes back to active parents who played tennis, badminton and golf. I was a normal boy who loved to kick a ball around and tennis clubs and cricket clubs provided a great holiday time environment for useful hours to be whiled away. My parents' love of sport extended to their faithfully standing on sidelines in all kinds of weather watching what must of been unusually boring activities on the field—though I didn't recognise how much love that took at the time. Beyond ball games, swimming and sailing led to a love of the water, which continues to this day.

Family vacations were often the centrepiece of the year where we would be all together, though often in very modest surroundings. Rented beach chalets were the usual accommodations, simple and basic—rich in terms of fun opportunities. The simplicity reached chemical loos and carrying water from the local well. Other vacations which were character forming were provided by farm work through school holidays which got one close to nature.

Running through all of these influences were girls. I knew they were different without necessarily understanding why or how. I was raised in a segregated environment where schools were not co-ed and even my home background was more of boys than girls. I definitely liked them and worked on it. My wife, Meriel, was a childhood sweetheart whom I abandoned at the age of twelve or thirteen having spent several weeks' pocket money on bringing her to the movies for no reward—not even a handholding outing. Many years later we did get together again.

My childhood was certainly not unhappy but could be said to represent small beginnings. I was privileged with the start I had in life, maybe a small "p" in privileged but I was given a great start, decent schooling, a work ethic and value systems to build on and love. Only my Maker would know whether I made the most of it. I often feel that I got a great deal more than I deserve.

No Place Like Home

Despite man's tendency to roam
When young no better place to be
Than in the safe embrace of home
The bosom of one's family

Roger Handy

Tact

The following are two stories from my very early youth. These are typical of stories from children which show what happens before they learn about such things as tact. They relate to a time when I was old enough to understand some things but too young to know the consequences.

My parents had left my older brother and myself down in Arklow with friends at the start of our summer holidays and went home to clear up and leave our rectory ready for visitors. Coming down the next day they sat us both down to tell us as gently as possible how, as our cat had become old and unwell, they had brought it to the vet and our cat was now asleep. Mum and Dad thought that they were dealing with the matter quite well and that their two boys were taking it without too much emotion. Not too many tears from big brother but the quizzical look from Roger spelt trouble, I had to know the details and finally upset the emotional balance by asking of the vet " and how did he dead it, did he shoot it?"

My lack of tact, hopefully because of my young age, showed itself again when my Aunt and Uncle called unexpectedly one Sunday near tea time. With nothing extra to feed more mouths (shops weren't open for food sales in those days) the relatively fresh 'brown square' loaf of bread was put on the table. Again all was going well until after another slice had been cut for my Aunt, Roger with a worried frown suggests that we shouldn't cut any more as that was the dog's food and he hadn't yet been fed!

Children, don't you love them!

Al Byrne

Children Bringing Up Children

Allowing for the fact that it is up to adults to help bring up children it is sometimes forgotten that children help to bring up adults. Not only that but it is up to children to help bring up other children!

Let me explain then how it came about that my sister Mary, when she was about two years old, was responsible for helping to teach me how to write stories when I was only nine years old.

There were five children in the Byrne home and I was the second eldest. Money was short and one of the great treats we got was when we were given four pence to go to the pictures in The Fountain picture house in James's Street on a Saturday afternoon. There we watched what was called "follyeruppers" or what is now called "soap operas". It was all about Cowboys and Indians — the goodies and the baddies — and we loved it. The snag was that I had to earn the fourpence and the only way to do that was to wheel my sister in her pram around and around the block for at least two hours to get us both from under my mother's feet. That act of pram-pushing was seen by us boyos as absolutely sissy stuff and we were most embarrassed at having to do it. Girls could do it and that was OK. But not boys.

But the thought of wondering what happened to Tom Mix and his chums since the previous Saturday was too great to bear so I did the pram-pushing. And then I discovered that another lad in the street named Tommy who also cared about

Tom Mix was not as lucky as I was because only now and again did he get four pence to go to the pictures. When he was out of luck he came to me to find out what happened. And then the deal was struck. If he walked with the pram and me pushing it I'd tell him all. Pushing a pram on your own is hell. Pushing it with a pal beside you and his hand on the handle is OK. We were on! My problem was that I had to spin out a twenty-minute follyerupper for the two-hour pram pushing. That's when I had to invent those extra bits never seen on screen. That's when I had to learn how to write stories.

Sometimes I made a mess of it and got it all muddled up and Tommy would spot it and query it. That meant extra creativity on my part as well as talking myself out of the literary mess I'd got into. Although I didn't know it at the time it made me assemble my facts in a more orderly way and also taught me how to avoid tedious repetition. I was a Charles Dickens in the making!

So from this long distance in time I go back to where I began this little piece of nostalgia and I thank a little boy of ten called Tommy for saving me from the charge of "sissy" and for making me think about so many facets of writing.

I also thank my sister Mary for once upon a time being only two years old and in need of pram-pushing and, at that time, for being sensible enough to indicate that, even with the best of story tellers, the audience is entitled to sleep through it all if they so decide.

It's all part of children bringing up children!

Maurice Abrahamson

Over Sixty-Six Years Ago

It is embarrassing to admit that I am an old boy of a girls' school. But there you are. Alexandra School, when situated in Earlsfort Terrace, had a nursery form for young ladies and young gentlemen. Rather, to be precise, in my time, three little boys and a horde of pretty girls. I was around five or six years old, it not being the practise in those days to be sent to crèches, when I joined that merry throng. I cannot remember what we were taught or how we spent the time. But, I thought one of the girls, in particular, was *very* pretty. I am happy to say that my judgement was good. She became a well-known film actress, and many years later, when I found myself at a party, at which she was one of the guests, I launched myself in her direction, gabbling away about Alexandra School. She remembered her time there very well but due to some reason or another, which I find inexplicable to this day, she could not quite recall my face.

It was around this time, that the twins were born. I can still envisage the scene in the room which I shared with my sister, Beth, when our father, Leonard, came and told us he had a big surprise for us. We jumped up and down on the bed, and then he informed us that we had two new brothers. We continued to jump and down, rather less enthusiastically, for usually when he talked of a surprise it turned out to be especially delicious chocolate bars.

There, I must confess, my little grey cells cease to conjure up the events which succeeded the birth of the twin boys on

29th October 1932. However, for the purposes of this contribution, perhaps I can relate them, with benefit of subsequent family chats and the copy of The Irish Times, dated 18th November, 1932, in our family album.

My mother, Tillie, gave birth in Portobello Nursing Home (now a College) and we lived in Fitzwilliam Place. Every evening, after the last of his patients had been seen, Dad would drive through Adelaide Road, up Charlemont Road and turn right just before the bridge where stood the Home. On the day in question, when he turned around the corner, he was horrified to see it engulfed in flames. The fire brigade had already arrived, and there was a crowd of onlookers. One of these rushed over to Dad's car, wrenched the car door open, and shouted "they're alright, they're alright", a kindness my father never, ever forgot.

But being "alright" was a pretty relative term, for although firemen had brought down to safety some twenty-four patients and two babies, they could do nothing for Mum. In the first place, they had been born very prematurely and were snuggled in wads of cotton wool and covered in olive oil. She refused to let one of the firemen take them down the ladder, fearing that they could not survive exposure to the cold air, and she refused point blank to leave them. The nurse, who was on duty, also refused to leave. She recounted how the electricity went out, how a fireman on one of the ladders said to blow out the candles which she had lit, because there was an escape of gas, and how awful was the feeling of being in total blackness while a fire raged around them.

After a couple of hours, the ordeal ended, when the firemen managed to get through to my mother's room and bring all of them to safety through the remains of the stairway. Shortly afterwards, there was a tremendous crash and the ceiling of the room collapsed.

By this little miracle my twin brothers Max and David, survived, and I have had to put up with them ever since.

Lucinda Jacob

Family Matters

Waking Dad

"Daddy, are you sleeping?" I asked, my chubby little fingers simultaneously pulling back an eyelid to check. No response. Next I jumped on his stomach and ... Panic! I'd burst my Daddy! All the air was rushing out of him with a terrible raspberry noise and he was going all saggy! I howled and then burst into tears of joyous relief as I realised he was pretending to be a balloon and trying not to laugh.

Waking The Baby

Staying with our fiercest aunt I came upon my younger sister sitting, looking collapsed and tearful, beside the empty pram.

"What's the matter?" I asked.
"She wanted to know did I wake the baby," she replied.
"But you weren't anywhere near it," I said, confused.
"I know." She sobbed, " I just said yes to see what would happen."

Much Older

Feeling worn out, and still a bit sleepy, driving down to Dun Laoghaire to leave my three year old to her crèche one morning, a little voice chirped up from the back seat:

"Mummy, when you were young,"
"Yes darling?"

"Mummy, when you were young did dinosaurs eat grass?"

Well that woke me up! Made me laugh too, as I searched for an answer less banal than the one that came to mind. But I did wonder how she thought I went back that far. She already knew Jesus was around really, really long ago and that dinosaurs were before him. I suppose him still being a baby at Christmas doesn't help. Cheered me up though, I'm not ancient, just all embracing in her eyes.

Ken Peare

Up To No Good

"Maggots, how did you worm your way in here" boomed the Colonel living on Clonkeen Road, when I dropped in to play snooker on his quarter-sized table. That was one of my less complimentary nicknames among others such as "Sparks" and "Smiler". We had recently moved to a small semi-detached on a long narrow road which my father had purchased for the princely sum of nine hundred pounds. Opposite was "Kitt's Field" named after a very ordinary but much loved pony, where we played our football matches, intermingled with "spin the bottle" in the local broken down shed. I think I preferred football at the time. The stomach churning suspense of who the bottle would point towards was sometimes more than fun. Losing a football match was often preferable to kissing a girl I never liked — quite an embarrassment at that age.

My first home was in 4 Woodland Avenue, where I lived with three older sisters, Mum, Dad and two aged aunts — Kathleen and Rose. They were a source of great amusement to my friends due to difficulties with their "S's and "R's". "Come and sit on my knee" became "Come and shit on my knee" — causing waves of raucous laughter all around.

My aptitude for getting a quart out of a pint pot was learnt at the tender age of eight when I went into business with my two hens which were cosseted in a small shed at the back of the garden. The eggs I sold to my mother, who was amazed at how prolific they were — nothing to do with the fact that there was a small farm nearby which kindly supplemented my layers from time to time.

I almost went blind from the natural curiosity of a little boy, a result of my poking a stick (too short by half) into a gently humming wasps' nest. I enraged them so much that they charged en masse, buzzing mercilessly around my grubby little face, using their venom to close one eye totally and put me to bed for a week.

My fixation with girls started not long after as I was riding down Merrion Avenue to St Philips and St James's National School. Suddenly there appeared two girls on one bike swerving from side to side — what a sight. In my excitement I jammed on both brakes, went straight over the handle bars and into hospital to have all my front teeth out. I have never forgotten the joy of having to live on Lustre canned pears and peaches, a real treat in those days, following this escapade.

We were very lucky to have one holiday a year, always the first two weeks in August, in the huts in Silver Strand, where the high pitched smell of the Elsan toilet remains with me today. My mother, what a marvellous woman, used to cook on a sawdust stove for the whole family and illumination was by gaslight. The stove was basically a biscuit tin full of smouldering sawdust with the heat coming through a funnel to cook the stew, which was so often part of our diet. The days were long, consisting of swimming, fishing off the rocks and walks to the lighthouse with my sisters and their boyfriends.

With three good looking sisters, there were always boys around and during the summer, they used to come to Belfield, a farm in Kilmacanogue where my Dad was brought up, to help with the hay-making. Wonderful memories of hanging on for dear life as we raced around the fields on the back of the lad's motorbikes, Beauty of Bath apples from the orchard, Mum's famous flans and lots and lots of people having fun. One abiding memory is that of my sister June, in a bedroom with one of her boyfriends, who shall be nameless. He wanted me to go and she wanted me to stay. "How much will you give me" I asked. The bidding started at a shilling and then finally, when she offered nine shillings, he topped it with ten. I pondered briefly on my decision and decided to take the ten bob note, knowing that everybody would be happy. My first big deal! As a pal of mine often says, "It would be hard to be this lucky again".

Bitter Sweet

Among the stories in this book
There seems no harm to tell a few
That have an introverted look
And give a moral point of view

Gordon Linney

Childhood Revisited

Many years ago, just coming up to Christmas, I was visiting a young man in prison who was serving a very long sentence. He came from far away and had no family or friends to visit him and his local clergy had asked me to make contact with him.

I had already visited him a number of times but on this occasion we got talking about the past, his home life and where he had grown up. Soon the conversation turned to Christmas and it quickly became obvious that this tragic young man had none of the memories or experiences of Christmas that many of us would take for granted. The circumstances of his early life were such that the possibility did not exist. His was a broken home, his parents had addiction problems and he and his siblings were always in trouble with the neighbours.... And the law!

I remember as I stepped out into the fresh air and as the prison gate slammed behind me being gripped by two distinct feelings. First of all my pity for the child in the man I had just left who had known so little joy or affection in those vital growing years that even Christmas was unknown territory to him. Secondly, I had an extraordinary sense of gratitude for those who had given me such a wonderful and happy childhood that it was difficult at times to know when Christmas began and when it ended. Indeed such was that feeling of gratitude that I felt I had to go, then and there, and revisit the old home we had left some forty years ago. And so I headed off, wondering as I went, how I would explain to the present owners the reason for my visit.

I arrived at the very familiar door and rang the bell. No response. I rang again, still no response. After several further attempts, I realised that there was no one at home. But I also realised something much more profound, namely that you cannot revisit your memories, you cannot re-enter the past. It is part of your present and with you wherever you are.

And the moral of the story? To give our children and grandchildren good memories that will stay with them for life and to be genuinely sensitive to those who have been deprived of them.

Sheila Boland

The 'Herald Boot Fund'

I am of a generation when the poor children of Dublin were not as well looked after as most are today. I lived on the Rathgar Road as a child, near the Rathmines end, and well remember that my feelings were touched when I saw other little ones in rags and bare footed, even in the snow; my eyes would fill with tears and I would give them the only thing I could as one child to another, my sweets and bars of chocolate. The "Herald Boot Fund" was inaugurated and thankfully their little blue feet were somewhat insulated from the cold and wet pavements. There was so much to do and so few people who cared enough - movements such as the "Cottage Home for Little Children" were manned by caring people of insight.

Dorothy Robbie

Trevor

It was only in retrospect that that particular Saturday afternoon in August 1939 was a special one. At the time it seemed as any other and yet, looking back, after that day nothing would ever be the same for us.

There were twelve of us who met that day, all in our mid teens and very full of our own importance. We were all Lower VI pupils at the local co-ed grammar school, we had known each other all through our school years and were well used to spending time together both in and out of school. In those long ago days, though we thought of ourselves as extremely sophisticated and adult, there was an innocence and naivety about us that would be laughable to most of today's teenagers. We girls fell in and out of love with one or other of the lads in the group and when a "relationship" broke up, it didn't seem to leave any ill-feeling.

We girls had our own hidden criteria to decide which lad was favourite "flavour of the month" and on the day in question, the boy we were all most interested in was Trevor.

Up to that summer he had been someone we had scarcely noticed. He had been a skinny bespectacled shy lad on his first day and no one seemed to have been aware of him changing. We tolerated him because of his friendship with Philip, one of the most popular lads.

But Sports Day in 1939 changed out minds. We suddenly realised that our school representative in the most prestigious race of all, the Inter-School Mile was none other than Trevor, who under our noses it seemed, had turned overnight into a golden haired Adonis.

We watched as Trevor kept up with the leaders to the last bend and then, as they came into the final straight, came away from the others to win.

From then on, through the rest of the term and into the holidays, Trevor became the centre of our interest. We teased him, we flirted with him and generally made much of him. He came out of his shell a little and had even begun to show a certain shy interest in Mary and she, in turn, had confessed to the rest of us girls that the feeling was mutual.

It had been decided after the usual desultory debate that we would go for a walk on one of the long hills that framed our South Wales valley. And so we had ambled along, chatting, arguing and fooling about until we found ourselves at the side of a huge, disused old reservoir. It had had a protective high wall around it but this had long ago fallen down in places. And so it was easy to get right up to the old rusting reservoir itself. It rose high above us and one of the lads, I forget which one, began climbing up the ladder attached to the side.

We watched him as he climbed very slowly. He reached the top, peered over the edge for a few seconds and then began the climb down. He muttered something about the ladder being a bit loose but that it was all right. Then another of the lads did the climb and than a third. Somehow without a word having been said the climb had turned into a sort of rite of passage for the boys. The last of the boys was Trevor but when it came to his turn he just said quietly "No. I'm not going up".

I remember there was moment's silence. Then a chorus of coaxing began but he remained adamant. Finally, David, who didn't like Trevor anyway, said "Don't be such a sissy. The rest of us have done it". Trevor shook his head and then someone muttered "Coward".

We started homewards. No-one seemed to feel much like talking. Trevor and Philip walked together a little apart from the rest of us. When we arrived at the Italian cafe which was our usual haunt, Trevor didn't come in but left on his own.

After he had gone, it seemed easier to talk. And the talk was all of the climb and Trevor's refusal to do it. Most of the boys and even some of the girls felt that he had been a coward and in some way had been found wanting. David in particular was scathing. Then suddenly Philip blew his top in anger. "You don't have a clue, the lot of you. He's not a bloody coward. He's got more guts than any of you. His Dad is dying of cancer and if Trev had fallen — as he could have — that bloody ladder was all but coming away — what the hell would his mother have done. He's all she's going to have left."

We went home soon after Philip's outburst. No-one mentioned the incident again. Term began, then the war started. We were never all together again. Trevor's Dad died. All the boys were called up and Trevor went into the Army. He was killed in France exactly one month after D-Day having been awarded an M.C. in the field.

Donald Caird

Till They Put Their Lives Back Together Again

The future was bright when they married
Shortly before the First World War.
He had a job with good prospects
She created a home they'd adore.
The village they lived in near Dublin
Had been home for years to their clan
They were surrounded by relations and neighbours
who all helped when the family came.
Most of the lads in the village were horsemen
When the horse bore the burden of war.
As the call came for their service
None felt inclined to withdraw.
With their horses they sailed out of Dublin
to the cheering crowds on the quays
but the prospect was different at Vincy
where they were bogged in mud to their knees.
The war they had trained for was past them
to give way to the car, to gas and the tank.
They were slaughtered in their thousands
irrespective of creed, or age or rank.
He returned home to the village a hero
but broken in health, unable to work
for long periods, declining in status and wealth.
There were now three kids in the family
the latest only two months old,
the mother showed signs of a fever

mistaken, alas! for a cold.
In days she was dead from the fever
diagnosed as the Spanish flu.
Leaving three children behind her
What now could her husband do?
With the help of his elderly mother
he could cope with the older two
but he had to seek help for the baby
as the village was wracked with the flu.
The wife of the rector came quickly
She'd been a friend of his wife
She knew that the Cottage Home for Little Children
could play a vital part in his life.
He met the widow of a man from his regiment
who had returned to the village to live.
In a year or two they had married,
both families now settled as one
the baby was now reunited thanks to the Cottage Home.

Mary Robinson

Rights Of The Child

In passing on her good wishes to the Cottage Home, the High Commissioner invited us to quote an extract from a statement made to an international gathering of young people at a ceremony commemorating the tenth anniversary of the adoption of the Convention of the Rights of the Child.

Geneva, 6 July 1999.

You young people come from all over the world. From Countries suffering from tremendous violence, from poor families and neighbourhoods forced to the margins of society. Some of you are fortunate to come from rich countries and peaceful neighbourhoods but which have their own hidden violence and exclusion.

You will tell us of your problems and those of your relatives and friends, but please also tell us of your joys. I am already aware of what some of you do for the cause of human rights. In Colombia you struggle for peace in a very violent society and members of Tapori share friendship and support with the poor and excluded in both rich and poor countries.

I must tell you that as I visit various countries as High Commissioner for Human Rights, I too learn first hand what it means to you to be a child or young person today.

In June I visited Russia and spent some time meeting with the young people of that country. I was told that the children there were asked where they feel their rights were not respected. Many replied: at school. Well, in one Russian school I went to I learned that the children, teachers and parents have together developed a list of Rules in School which sets out the rights and responsibilities of all. On the basis of this, they have organised their own school ombudsman to supervise the observance of these rules and to mediate when children feel their rights are being violated. This is a good example of how children can be actively involved in knowing and protecting their own and others' rights.

Unfortunately, many children do not yet enjoy even the most basic rights. In Kosovo last week I met children whose homes had been destroyed so they had nowhere to live. Some had had relatives killed. I visited a camp where members of the Roma community had no clean water and disease was rampant. Such conditions are the daily lot of many children.

Ten years ago, all the countries agreed without dissent, that children have rights and they have a duty to protect them.

And how these rights were presented was revolutionary. The starting point was that you children were full human beings with a right to participate in your own development; you have your opinions and the right to voice them.

What does the Convention say? First it says that whether you come from a rich or poor family, regardless of your gender, your country or religion, language or colour, you are all equal and have an equal right to protection under the Convention.

The basic rights are to life, survival and development, which are perhaps the rights most often violated. Then there is the right to participate in decisions affecting you; the right to have your say, as mentioned earlier.

You have the right to be with your parents, to education and health, to protection from dangers such as drugs, sexual and economic exploitation and harmful work. And you have the right to be treated fairly by Courts and the police.

Also you have the right to rest and play and take part in cultural and artistic activities. But you still have to do your homework.

There are other rights in the Convention, but even going by those I have just listed, very few children can say they enjoy them all, and many millions enjoy very few, or none at all.

At the last session of the Commission on Human Rights, attention was focussed on the marginalization and exclusion of children and emphasis was placed on the fact that children were not taken into account in macro-economic policy formulations.

Integrating child rights into economic policy formulations will require advocacy and research. But I believe as we succeed the lives of children in developed and developing countries will be measurably improved. And the Convention on the Rights of the Child provides a universally agreed standard against which to measure progress.

I look forward to working with the Council and the participating agencies in defining the macro-economic implications of the Convention and identifying ways to adjust policy to promote greater respect for the rights of children.

Bartley Sheehan

Autobiography in Five Short Verses

There's A Hole in My Sidewalk
By Portia Nelson

I

I walk down the street
There is a deep hole in the sidewalk.
I fall in.
I am lost ... I am helpless.
It isn't my fault.
It takes forever to find a way out.

II

I walk down the same street.
There is a deep hole in the sidewalk.
I pretend I don't see it.
I fall in again.
I can't believe I am in the same place.
But is isn't my fault.
It still takes a long time to get out.

III

I walk down the same street.
There is a deep hole in the sidewalk.
I see it is there.

I still fall in. It's a habit.
My eyes are open.
I know where I am.
It is my fault.
I get out immediately.

IV

I walk down the same street.
There is a deep hole in the sidewalk.
I walk around it.

V

I walk down another street.

John De Courcy Ireland

Remembering Granny from Galway

Little Granny from Galway, with your lovely silver-white hair and its streak of gold at the back! Dad, your son, whom I would never know, had taken mother to the other end of the world, where a cruel war would make him a victim and prevent her for years from coming home, left me with you to look after me. You never spoke an angry word. What you would not like we did not do, my two cousins also in your care and I, because to offend anyone as kind as you was unthinkable. You taught us to read a lot and walk a lot, and your house was a house of peace and simple joy, where you sang us hush songs, you told us strange sayings from every corner of the land, like "Lough Neagh bones, Lough Neagh bones, put them in sticks and take them out stones" and "from Carickmascross to Crossmaglen you meet more thieves than honest men".

Only once in all those magic years did you seem upset — when you had heard that Michael Collins had been shot.

Then one day you put a ticket and a mysterious document called a passport recently acquired around my neck and told me I must find my way to Rome where my mother and my stepfather, whom she had just married, were living. She said to take a good look at Normandy from the train, it was like the family's ancestral Kildare.

I was eleven. That day my childhood ended, I stepped into a new world of bustle, noise and feuds, hatreds and pleasures, and always absorbing interest. I have never known again the profound peace, the joy and the trust of my Granny from Galway's house, but the feel of it I can never lose.

Christmas Capers

Now children it's the Christmas season
A favourite time, if you believe
And there was always special reason
To do just that on Christmas Eve!

Hugh Leonard

About Christmas

The cliché will not go away and lose itself. Only think of Christmas, and there is an image of childhood. The great trip by tram with my mother; the visit to Santy, who mysteriously contrived to be in so many shops, so many Toylands, at once: — Pim's, Clery's, Kellett's, Switzer's and Brown Thomas's. We did not blink at this ubiquity, for magic was our everyday coinage. I remember most vividly the little money-cups, flying to-and-fro on wires far above the shop counters. The once-a-year lunch in Pim's, daring in its extravagance at two-and-thruppence — in later, posher years, afternoon tea at the Ritz or Claridge's was not its equal.

Then, at home on Christmas Eve, the grate new-blacked and the fire blazing and fierce, regardless of cost. The dusting off and the putting up of the decorations that swooped and rose in great multicoloured chains, converging like old cronies in the middle of the kitchen. And there was the opening-out into its full splendour of a great paper bell, where the chains met. Sprigs of holly were set behind what Dylan Thomas would one day call the "dicky-bird-watching pictures of the dead". Other sacred rituals were the plucking and stuffing of the turkey, my father polishing every shoe and boot in the house, until the very wall-pictures were reflected in the pools of their blackness.

And of course there was the day itself. There is a memory of blinking awake in the great double bed, the room pitch black except for a small glow in the grate from last night's cinders. You reached upwards with a daring hand to the bed-rail behind, first encountering the crinkling smoothness of wrapping paper; then tracing a shape with one's fingers. A book? A gun? A game? Next, the walk with my father to early mass, out breaths visible before us in the cold air. The other worshippers, hurrying silently, dim figures in the dark — I would see the same people, years later in *The Hunters in the Snow* by Bruegal. Then back home for the great breakfast; dipping frugally into the *Hotspur, Adventure* or *Film Fun* annuals, careful not to devour them too greedily.

Next, there was the visit from bowler-hatted Mr. Quirke next door ("God save all here!"), in quest of his yearly bottle of stout, I still see the froth on his white moustache and even now feel a remembered twinge of resentment, for to me he was an interloper not part of the Christmas that was jealously ours. When he was gone — after his wife Essie had twice thumped on the wall — there was dinner: turkey and ham — and for once I ate and almost liked the detested Brussels sprouts — and the dark pudding studded with fruits in its moat of custard.

The great day moving inexorably towards its close; the falling of night, the coming of my uncle John and aunt Chris to eat biscuits, drink port wine from Gilbeys at the corner and play 25s. Down the years I can hear the tinkling, affected little laugh of my aunt, who had married a paper-keeper, the lowest form of civil service life. She was on that account the Hyacinth Bucket, pronounced Bouquet, of the family.

Christmas for poor people was a nailing of colours to the mast. It was a shout that proclaimed survival. Another year had been safely lived. My parents were wise in their ignorance. They had never learned a word of poetry in their lives. And yet they knew, with Blake:

Man was made for joy and woe,
And when this we rightly know,
Thro' the World we safely go.

I have written about all this many a time, not because it is a convenient cliché, but because, cosy and nostalgic as it may seem, it is the truth, and now, as Sam Goldwyn is alleged to have said, what we need are some new clichés. Nowadays, the magic has thinned out. The conjuring trick has been done too often.

And yet for many years my wife and I have been no less willing prisoners of tradition. With our daughter, home from London, we have driven to Kerry every December 23rd and in whatever weather, always to stay in the same hotel. We greet that same Dutch foursome every year. We again wonder whether a certain bluff Englishman is wearing his own hair or the most outrageous of wigs. We listen to the same pianist

117

playing the same sing-along favourite. After midnight on Christmas Eve, we exchange presents upstairs under our tree, and next day we walk the silent hills, each wearing a new jacket, or gloves or scarf. '

On being asked to write this brief piece, I for once strive to give my own past a rest. Instead, I turn my mind to our daughter's Christmases and how she may one day look back on them. One can only guess, of course. When she was small, we spent the holiday itself at home. In the afternoon, our friends G---- and B---- would come with their son and five small daughters, who squeezed on to our sofa and stared, hypnotised, at the television. Next day or the day after, my wife, Danielle and I flew to Jamaica, Grenada, Antigua, Barbados — a hellhole in its stuffiness — and Young Island, off the coast of St. Vincent, which was our favourite.

With the years, the pattern changed, and nowadays, Danielle, who lives in London uncomplainingly comes home — it is our home, of course, no longer hers — and there is the excitement of waiting at the airport for the magic word "Landed" to appear on the arrivals screen. When the three of us drive to Kerry, she takes over the wheel at the half-way mark — Birdhill, perhaps or Cashel. I underwent a cardiac by-pass close on six years ago, and there is a pretence that I must not over-exert myself — actually, I love driving, but we play the game of the enfeebled pa and the caring sprig. We are not natural huggers or maulers, our mutual affection is a vast subterranean lake, and this is one of the small ways it seeks and finds the surface.

And we are conscious that Dan's ties with "home" have become fewer. Her real life is elsewhere, and a few times each year she leaves that life to make us the gift of herself. It is, although she would not for an instant think of it as such, our Christmas present. We argue, share jokes, get new insights, enjoy each other; and I find a small delight in simplicities such as making tea in the morning and bringing it to her room.

I wonder if in the future, near or far, she will be asked to write a thousand words for a book of "Childhood Memories". And, if so, what form will they take? They will be clear-eyed and unsentimental, whatever else. When I wrote a play called *Da,* which was a memoir of my parents and myself, it was commonplace for some youngish man to tell me, by letter or face to face, that he identified with the son in the play — that is, he saw it was a portrait of his own father. I was privately amused that he never thought of it the other way about, as a father remembering his son.

What goes around comes around. We all of us have to change roles

Dorothy Kilroy

Santa's Triumph

I was five years old and Europe was being torn apart by World Ward II. Although Ireland was not officially involved, the ravages of the war still affected her. There were shortages of almost everything. Grown-ups huddled over the wireless anxiously listening to each news bulletin, hoping to hear that it would all soon be over.

At that time we lived with my grandmother and several unmarried aunts and uncles. One of the kitchen drawers housed a small pile of ration books filled with coupons which could be exchanged for a limited amount of tea, sugar and butter per person per week. Coupons were also required in order to purchase clothes, and I vaguely remember a time when an aunt was to be married, how family and friends donated some of their precious coupons so that she might have a respectable trousseau.

There was no coal available and high columns of turf were erected to dry in the passage outside the kitchen. The only warm room in the house was the kitchen where the range was kept burning all the time. We were dressed in chill proof vests and liberty bodices to keep out the cold. Mealtimes produced hearty dishes like stew with dumplings and jam roly-poly.

All of this went over my head. Life had never been any different. But Christmas was coming, and although I was too young to really understand, some instinct told me that things were hard to come by. Money was short and shops had limited supplies.

What I really wanted was a doll's pram. My mother helped with the note to Santa. It was put up the chimney where it must soon have reeked with the smell of turf. And then I waited.

On Christmas Eve I was put to sleep in my mother's big bed. I can still instantly recall the intense feeling when I awoke next morning. Santa had done very well indeed with the limited resources at his disposal. A packet of crayons, balloons, new pennies, a colouring book — but instead of placing them in the stocking at the foot of the bed, he had cleverly laid them on the pillow all around my head, giving the impression that one was waking up in Wonderland itself.

And then — Oh joy! Oh rapture! — in front of the dressing table stood the doll's pram. It was blue and white and quite perfect. I learned many years later that Santa had procured it by answering an advertisement in the newspaper placed by a couple in Donegal whose family had grown too old for it. It is amazing what a spot of lick and polish can do. Other Christmases have come and gone but that one in the 1940s somehow stands out above them all.

CLAIRE M

Chris De Burgh

An African Christmas Stocking

When I was nearly seven years old, I went as a boarder to Aravon School in Bray, for my parents were living at that time in Nigeria. When the Christmas holidays finally arrived, my brother and I flew the DC3s and Argonants of B.E.A. to Lagos, where our parents met us and brought us to our rented home. I remember being fascinated by the smells, sights and sounds of Africa, in particular the market places, seething with life and colour, from the dresses and shawls of the black women to the exotic vegetables and wares for sale.

On Christmas Eve, however, it began to occur to me that Santa may not be able to make it down to Africa and our house, not only because of the significant distance from Lapland but also because of the wild and massive tropical storm that was raging all around us, with claps of thunder that illuminated the countryside for miles, trees and buildings leaping out of the darkness as the lightening brought them to life. But my fears about Santa were groundless, for the African dawn revealed, at the end of our beds, sack-fulls of goodies that had been thoughtfully brought to us from the North Pole — succulent African fruits, wooden carvings of elephants and crocodiles, strange African coins with holes in the middle, and a wild array of sweets, nuts, dates and chocolates — all consumed with gusto in that African winter wonderland!

A Few Good Sports

All children have a sporting chance
And games are part of childhood's scheme
While some through sport in life advance
Success for some remains a dream

Ken Haughton

Finding One's Feet

I have two vivid memories that stand out in my mind today as clearly as at the time that they happened. The first was when I cannot have been more then four years old and thought that a pond covered in duck weed would be a lovely place on which to run, only to be saved before disappearing under by my father who fortunately was with me. I can still picture the shiny green surface.

The second memory, many years later, was my first international hockey match. For the first five or so minutes the ball whizzed around at a pace that I had never experienced, even at inter-provincial level. I remember being almost panic stricken, feeling out of my depth. Subsequently, I settled down and actually scored twice!

From the experience of that day I have always held the strong view that anyone appointed to be a selector at any sport should have had the experience of participating at the level for which they are selecting teams or individuals.

John Treacy

Silver Lining

Memories of the Los Angeles Olympic Games Marathon and the welcome distraction of childhood innocence from daughter Caoimhe who was totally unaware of what was going on.

August 12th 1984.

8.15 a.m., and only forty-five minutes to get my breakfast and pack my bag before the car arrives to take me to U.C.L.A. As I dress I take a quick look out the window to see the bright sun reflecting on the water in the swimming pool. It is going to be eighty-five degrees Fahrenheit today according to the weather forecast on T.V. last night. I am relieved, as it could have been over one hundred.

My daughter Caoimhe arrives into the bedroom, full of fun and happiness. She has helped me so much to forget about the Olympic Games in L.A. over the last five days since the disappointment of having run so poorly in the final of the 10,000 metres. Caoimhe, totally unaware of what is going on, brings me into her own world of dogs, Sesame Street and sunshine. As I watch her climb onto the bed, I know that she and my wife, Fionnuala, will be my inspiration when I need it most.

My breakfast consists of tea, toast, polycose and gato load. Chuck, my driver, arrives early and we are off at 9.00 a.m. with the Los Angeles Times under my arm, a flask of coffee and my running gear. As Fionnuala and Caoimhe give me a hug of farewell, I realise that I am about to run the most important race of my life. There is no turning back now.

I arrive at the Olympic Village at 9.30 a.m., still seven and a half hours before the race. The waiting is hard despite having the company of Jerry Kiernan and Dick Hooper plus a few hundred telexes from well-wishers throughout Ireland.

Finally, it is time to put on the racing gear, pack the bag and catch the bus to the check in and starting area at Santa Monica. I find a bench in the check-in gym where I can rest my legs and pin on my numbers. Beside me is Carlos Lopes who I consider to be one of the favourites. We glance at each other without saying anything. At five minutes to race time I finally leave the coolness of the gym and, though drawn in row eight, edge my way up to row two of the starting line up.

The race starts off surprisingly fast and I find myself at the back of the field, running wide and carefully so as to avoid getting knocked over. As we get to the 2.5K mark and near to the first sponge station I have moved up a little to within about thirty yards of the leaders. Every time I reach for a sponge someone else gets there before me and I pass the station without a sponge. I decide I have to move through the field to ensure that I get my water bottle at the 5K mark. I get to the next station in about thirtieth position and although my bottle is gone I manage to grab the one intended for Jerry Kiernan and take up position beside Salazar, the home favourite. The roar of the crowd is deafening and there are American flags everywhere. As we reach 15K I have moved up to about fifteenth position and by 18K Ron Dixon and I have caught the leaders. I can't believe how good I feel.

For about the next 15K the lead bunch remains very large but then some of the big names start dropping back and the Englishman, Spedding, makes his move with just Nzau, Lopes and myself for company.

At 37K Lopes makes his decisive move. I have to let him go. Nzau starts to drop back and I begin to realise I will get a medal but which kind. At 41K I make my move for second and enter the coliseum tunnel seven yards ahead. Spedding comes back at me and I have to sprint with everything I've got. The line is finally in sight, only twenty yards to go, what a relief it is over. I raise my arms, I've got the silver.

It was exactly midnight when I got back to the house, proudly sporting my silver medal. It was easy to tell that the party was already in full swing. Fionnuala was at the door to greet me and we hugged, sharing the joy, after sharing so many failures. Meanwhile Caoimhe was where I probably should have been, snuggled up in bed with her own special thoughts and dreams. For her no great weight of expectation, no agony or ecstasy of failure or success, just the simple joy and innocence of childhood.

Christy O'Connor Junior

Just Like Childhood

The only certainty in Golf, like business (or childhood), is uncertainty, the only constant is change.

Quotes And Notes

Some memories are stories told
Some memories are anecdotes
Some tears , some laughs, from young and old
In rhymes or poems or famous quotes

Ronnie Appleton

A Favourite Quote

"The greatest pleasure I know is to do a good action by stealth, and to have it found out by accident."

Charles Lamb (1775-1834)

Marie Elaine Grant

'The Fiddler of Dooney' is one of my favourite childhood poems. This poem had a special meaning and significance when I was brought to see the lovely copper sculptures created by Imogen Stuart to commemorate the opening of the Stillorgan Shopping Centre in 1966. When seeing the beautifully carved fiddler and the three figures which resembled the people who danced on the Wave of the sea, this poem, 'The Fiddler of Dooney' became alive. To this day, when I visit the Stillorgan Shopping Centre and I pass by the lovely copper sculptures, I am immediately reminded of my favourite childhood poem.

The Fiddler of Dooney
by William Butler Yeats

When I play on my fiddle in Dooney
Folk dance like a wave of the sea;
My cousin is priest in Kilvarnet,
My brother in Mocharabuiee.

I passed my brother and cousin,
They read in their books of prayer;
I read in my book of songs,
I bought at the Sligo fair.
When we come at the end of time,
To Peter sitting in state.

He will smile on the three old spirits,
But call me first through the gate.

For the good are always the merry,
Save by an evil chance,
And the merry love the fiddle,
And the merry love to dance.

And when the folk there spy me,
They will all come up to me,
With "Here is the fiddler of Dooney!"
And dance like a wave of the sea.

John Quinn

*I enclose a poem I wrote some years ago about growing up in a
Co. Meath village in the 1940s and '50s. The village was
Ballivor and there was a saying about it "Goodnight Ballivor,
I'll sleep in Trim!" (Origin unknown and none too
complimentary!). I use it as a refrain at the end of each verse. I
feel it gives a flavour of rural Ireland of that period and for that
reason it may suit your book. The reference to 'Sam' in Verse 7
concerns Meath winning their first All-Ireland Football
Championship (Sam Maguire Cup) in 1949!*

Goodnight Ballivor

In Joe McLoughlin's General Stores
(or as the signboard said: General Joe McLoughlin – Stores)
They sold Indian meal and Women drawers,
Rat-traps, rashers and six-inch nails
Pints of porter, stout and ales.
Oh goodnight Ballivor … I'll sleep in Trim!

Master Conway held sway in the village school
He taught us to rhyme and he taught us to rule
We froze in our desks as to Algebra we aspired
But we thawed out again as we read by the fire.
Oh goodnight Ballivor …

And the little townlands all around
I sing the music of their sound
Muchwood, Shanco, the Hill of Down

132

Portlester, Glack and Carronstown.
Oh goodnight Ballivor ...

The law was enforced by Sergeant Quinn
For whom unlighted bikes were the greatest sin
The people's crimes kept his notebook full
Of uncut thistles and unlicensed bulls.
Oh goodnight Ballivor ...

We cut the turf in Coolronan bog
Spread it, footed it — an awful slog
But 'twas a day off school, so there was no hurry
And we rode home in style in Jim Rickard's lorry.
Oh goodnight Ballivor ...

In his forge the genial blacksmith Bill Kelly
Crouched beneath a horse's belly
Amid sparks and steam and smut and smoke
He hammered and turned and shaped a joke.
Oh goodnight Ballivor ...

And do you remember the September of '49
When we brought home 'Sam' for the very first time
Oh Cavan's Mick Higgins never tried his tricks on
When faced by our own Stonewall Dixon.
Oh goodnight Ballivor ...

At endless Mass on Easter morning
Fr. Farrell intoned the dues with warning
'One shilling each the following — Thomas Dunne,
    Moyfeigher'
While the oblivious Eugene Leddy de-waxed his ears.
Oh goodnight Ballivor ...

And once there came from out of the sky
A mysterious German spy
He came not to plunder not to pillage
But said on seeing our sleepy village:
Oh goodnight Ballivor, Ich schlafe in Trim!

To Sherrock's Garage we trudged through snow
To see Sikey Dunne's Great Picture Show
And frozen to all an oil-pocked seat
We basked in James Cagney's White Heat.
Oh goodnight Ballivor ...

Oh fair days for a few bob we minded cattle
And looked important with ash-plant and prattle
A deal was done with slapping of hands
And we bought Peggy's Leg from McGovern's van.
Oh goodnight Ballivor ...

And when I come to the end of my days
Be it natural causes or nuclear haze!
Whatever awaits in eternity –
My last words will surely be
(Even if I'm the sole survivor)
OH GOODNIGHT WORLD , I'LL SLEEP IN BALLIVOR

Barbara Robinson Smyth

Tea Pots and Bibles

When we were younger at children's parties it was obligatory to have a party piece, I was never a good singer so my party piece complete with all the actions was:

"I'm a little tea-pot, short and stout,
Here is my handle, here is my spout,
When the tea is ready, hear me shout
Tip me over pour me out".

The best part was the end bit!

*

My second contribution is on a more spiritual level and is from the Old Testament, Ecclesiastes 3:1 - 8

There is a time for everything and a season for every activity under heaven,

A time to be born and a time to die,
A time to plant and a time to uproot,
A time to kill and a time to heal,
A time to tear down and a time to build.
A time to weep and a time to laugh,
A time to mourn and a time to dance,
A time to scatter stones and a time to gather them.
A time to embrace and a time to refrain,
A time to search and a time to give up,
A time to keep and a time to throw away,

A time to tear and a time to mend,
A time to be silent and a time to speak,
A time to love and a time to hate,
A time for war and a time for peace.

*With the modern pace of life and our desire for instant everything **now** I think the above reading has a sense of balance and helps us through life's ups and downs which we all experience.*

Mary Henry

A Child's Garden Of Verses

Bed in Summer
by Robert Louis Stevenson

In winter I get up at night
And dress by yellow candle-light
In summer, quite the other way,
I have to go to bed by day.

I have to go to bed and see
The birds still hopping on the tree,
Or hear the grown-up people's feet
Still going past me in the street.

And does it not seem hard to you,
When all the sky is clear and blue,
And I should like so much to play,
To have to go to bed by day?

In this poem, Robert Louis Stevenson summed up perfectly my exasperation as a child at having to go to bed, in daylight, during the summer. There was far too much to be done to waste time lying seething in bed.

We lived just outside Cork city in an area which was then countryside and is now the end of the Lee Tunnel and a housing estate. The river and the countryside were our adventure playground. Our house was built in an old orchard and we children built our houses in the trees. We built rafts to go on the river and terrify my mother who during the summer holiday would knit our hated woollen vests! We had dogs, cats, a donkey I bought for five shillings, and my father's lovely ponies which we brought to pony shows. His ponies won prizes everywhere, even at the Royal Dublin Society. With so much to deal with who would want to go to sleep?

Just Memories

Despite life's many anxious times
There's many a fond memory
Told in these stories, quotes and rhymes
Of childhood 'Between you and me'.

Margaret Thompson

The Children

My daughter Caroline, who was about five years old, had the terrier on a lead and I heard a plaintive voice saying "Don't go so fast, Tim — you've got four legs and I've only got two!"

My son Christopher was three-and-a-half at the time. We were hurrying home from shopping on a wet afternoon. The buggy (then known as a push-chair) was heavy with child and shopping and I was in no mood to linger. As we passed a high wall Christopher asked "What's over that wall?" "Nothing" I said. "But I want to see".

But there's nothing to see". "But I want to *see* nothing to see". A curiosity and an unwillingness to accept an explanation without testing it himself that remained with him all his life.

David Norris

The Wrong Age

It is a funny thing but I never seem to have been the right age. At least as far as other people were concerned. When I was formerly categorised as a child, people frequently said to me "Oh you are far too young to do that". Now they are more inclined to say "Aren't you a little bit old for that?". Nevertheless I decided for myself that the ideal age for me was eighteen. As a result I decided at the age of six *to be* eighteen. I have been eighteen ever since. My eighteenth year was in fact so good after it finally came that I have extended it for the last thirty-seven years. I always regarded that rigid boundary line separating the child and the adult as rather artificial. I hope that we all keep something of the child with us.

I have always said that my life was spoiled by having had a happy childhood. If I had been wretchedly unhappy I might have written a tortured masterpiece like James Joyce. I am possessed however of a naturally happy nature which has limited my pretensions to genius. What constituted this happiness? Well first of all I had a lovely placid and witty mother. She didn't over indulge us but she provided for us a secure context. My pleasures as a child included gardening. I was given a little plot of my own in our back garden in Ballsbridge and enthusiastically planted rows of little bulbs of hyacinths and narcissus etc. and clumps of bachelor's buttons. My problems as a gardener however was that I was over enthusiastic and a trifle impatient. I remember my mother's mild reproof when she found me digging up all the plants I had carefully set the previous day in order to see whether their roots had grown. This is not something recommended by professional gardeners.

We were lucky enough to live on the borders of Ballsbridge and Sandymount. At that stage our neighbourhood was very keen to have Ballsbridge, Dublin 4 as a postal address as it had more cachet than Sandymount. Nowadays I gather the roles are reversed and Sandymount is quite the place to be. It was always a pleasure. It had a really village atmosphere with a cluster of old shops, nowadays, alas all gone. There was Frosts the newsagents, where you could buy your comics Dandy, Beano, or the Eagle from England with its wonderful oily magazine smell and bright illustrations of Dan Dare. Frost's also stocked munitions for infant weapons, cap guns, water pistols, stink bombs etc. On the corner was Batts chemist shop with its wonderfully angled door, reminiscent of a wild west saloon, and across the road Leverett and Fryes. In those days there were two grocery chains in Sandymount Leverett and Fryes and Findlaters. Both had sawdust strewn on the floor, tins of broken biscuits, vegetables, cheese, groceries, spices and most wonderful of all a machine with a handle and plenty of wires which sent your change whizzing across the ceiling from the counter to the cash desk and back again, when a handle was pulled.

My father died when I was six and I remember the tears in the dining room when my mother brought myself and my brother in to tell us the news. I regret to say that for this flood of emotion I was only able to squeeze out a single tear, as I didn't really understand what the loss of a father meant. My real tears came a week later when I learnt that we would no longer have a car.

We had very nice neighbours and I am still friendly with one of them after fifty years. Michael Moran, whom I have known since I was in my pram. Inevitably of course there were squabbles even among friends such as Michael and myself. I recall one day playing in the sand pit in Michael's garden, with our dinky toys, when a dispute arose over the possession of a prized Foden lorry. I am sorry to recall we reached a level of low sectarian abuse. At one point Michael stuck his tongue out, blew a raspberry and said "Yah, you are not even a Catholic". I went home in floods of tears to my mother, who said, "What's wrong dear?" to which I replied sniffling, "Michael Moran says I am not a Catholic". Calm as ever she responded "Of course you are, dear. Don't you say it every Sunday in Church, I believe in one Holy, Catholic and Apostolic Church. You are just not part of the Roman error like Michael". Full of glee I went back to Michael, stuck my tongue out and said "I am so a Catholic, ya, and just not part of the Roman error like you". I didn't quite know what the Roman error was but I knew it would cause trouble!

In those far off days of the '50s our pleasures were modest but to us greatly exciting. Off we went on the old steam train from Sandymount halt to Dun Laoghaire baths. Into the carriage clutching our cardboard ticket, bouncing around on the horse hair seats, throwing our bathing togs and towels up onto the net rack, above which were gloomy pictures of the Great Southern Hotel, Parknasilla, before letting down the leather strap opening the window to stick our heads out and get inevitably a smut in the eye. At Dun Laoghaire we would buy sixpenny slabs of Cleaves Toffee, guaranteed to remove every filling in your head. Then the lovely salty atmosphere of the white washed baths.

In the evening we might trundle along the path beside the railway line to the old Ritz Cinema in Serpentine Avenue to see a film such as 'The Rise and Fall of Legs Diamond'. On the way home we were all gangsters, machine gunning stray cats and screeching round corners in imaginary Buicks and Dodges.

Then there were the model planes, made out of balsa wood kits bought in Elvery's shop in Dublin. Back we came from town on the bus with our little packages and soon we were sticking our fingers to everything with the airplane glue, weeping in frustration over broken struts of balsa wood and innocently inhaling the fumes of the airplane dope. Occasionally these miracles of engineering did manage to fly.

Then there were the crazes. Hula hoops, skates, collecting vintage jazz records, running off to the Spring Show to collect any God's quantity of free samples, souvenir brochures, information about white scour, hoose and other assorted bovine ailments. Over the tractors and milking machines we clambered noisily, laughing guiltily when a large boar rolled over exposing pink genitalia or squealing with delight at parent's embarrassment when stallions pissed noisily on the cobble stones.

One of our great pleasures was being driven by Mrs. Moran (a figure of supreme elegance to us) in the Moran's lovely old pearl grey Austin A40 Somerset with its curved body line and registration, which I can still remember ZO

1588, out to watch what we called the BNI boat leave at 8.25 p.m. for the mysteries of Liverpool.

We ourselves did not travel quite so far abroad but I do remember one exhausting expedition when we cycled all the way to Glendalough. Down at Laragh I came across a huge clump of what to me then were very exotic blooms indeed, rhododendrons. I picked an arm full of these for my mother and cycled all the way back to Dublin with them precariously clutched to my bosom. I expected my mother to be delighted, in fact she was horrified at the risk to which I had exposed myself. Of such are the memories of childhood made.

Gloria Hunniford

Ambition

Being involved with working in the Television Industry on a daily basis, some of my childhood thoughts go back to the excitement of seeing television for the first time. We had a neighbour in Portadown where I grew up, called Mrs. McCracken and she lived literally a few yards from my home. As a family we didn't have that much spare money so a television set was totally out of the question. However, when Mrs. McCracken got a "new set" I was never away from her door. This box sitting in pride of place in the sitting room was the talk of the neighbourhood and the envy of many.

I remember I had to really stretch up to reach the big brass knocker and I'm sure there were times she wanted to totally ignore my pleading eyes and voice, but she to her credit, always let me in to watch whatever was on at the time. My big fascination strangely enough was "Come Dancing", not for the whirling around the floor, but for the swirling of the skirts. As a semi-professional singer from the age of eight, I could only afford roughly a dozen silver sequins on the frill around the neck of my yellow taffeta dress, so I couldn't believe that these dancers had hundreds of layers of tulle and zillions of sequins which twinkled every time they moved a satin shoe clad foot. Is it any wonder that for most of my professional life I have had a wardrobe with its fair share of rhinestones and glitter. They come and go with fashion, but you know what, they will never disappear totally, nor will my memories of those early programmes and the generosity of Mrs. McCracken to this star struck kid.

Hubert Wine

A Certain Career

When I was eight years old, I remember very clearly what made me want to do law. I read the headline in the Irish Newspaper "Hauptmann to Fry To-day". He was Bruno Hauptmann "the alleged" killer of the famous Lindbergh baby — he was convicted purely on circumstantial evidence; he was strapped into the electric chair twice, and, reprieved at the last moment on each occasion. The third time he was electrocuted. Strangely enough the case has come to light again some seventy years later and there has been a lot of doubt as to his guilt.

John Galsworthy, the famous author, once said, and I quote: "There is nothing more tragic in life than the impossibility of undoing what one has already done." In court, I remember quoting this in a particular case, but, adding a converse, "there is nothing more wonderful in life, than being given the opportunity to undo what has already been done".

Hilary Pratt

The Sun Always Shone

I had a blissful childhood in Sandycove during the War. We did not miss chocolate or imported fruits that we had never known, or for that matter, cars. The sea and the rocks were our playground and, of course, the sun always shone!

One Easter, our parents procured three chocolate animals. My brother and I devoured ours, marvelling in the new exotic taste, but our sister was a hoarder and her chocolate hen was stowed away.

Soon after she was invited to spend a few days with our grandparents in Blackrock, an adventure that involved a tram journey on her own.

A small bag was packed, pyjamas, toothbrush, shoes and a book. We watched casually, lest over-interest might alert suspicion. With noses glued to an upstairs window, we saw her leave the house, a small figure carrying a bag. She turned to wave, rounded the corner and was gone!

With one shout "She's left it behind!" we bounded to the cupboard. There is was, nestling in its soft wrapping beside the china doll with which she never played — her chocolate hen.

Partners in crime, we shared it equally, savouring every delicious crumb.

Retribution? I'm sure there was but I have forgotten it along with all the rainy days that there must have been too in that wonderful childhood.

One thing is certain, it didn't cure her of hoarding. She became a collector of antiques and fills her house with objet d'art and curios of the rarest sort. I have even spied a hen — of the porcelain variety of course.

Michael J. Earley

The 'Olden Days'

My Mother, who was in her thirties at the time, used to see me to bed.

I looked forward to that special time when I would hear a story from her own childhood - farmhouse holidays, lazy days, cut knees, the three sisters, with magic words like Tibradden, Tymon Lodge, Glencree, all referred to as taking place during the 'olden days'.

Life moves on.

I am now teased by towering teenagers and asked: "What was it like Dad when everything was black and white? When did it turn into colour?"

When you were born, I reply!

Louise Mansfield

Sandycove Days

Days filled with sunshine,
building sandcastles, fishing the rock pools
and going-home buckets filled with periwinkles.

The A to Z of Contributors

Between You and Me is sprinkled with contributions from a wide spectrum of Irish Society. Alphabetically speaking, it includes **Archbishop** Donald Caird, **Archdeacon** Gordon Linney, **artist** Louise Mansfield and **authors** (some are playwrights, journalists and illustrators too) such as Sheila Boland, Don Conroy, Margrit Cruickshank, Lucinda Jacob, Jennifer Johnston, Hugh Leonard, Julie Parsons, Anne Schulman and the Vineys, Eithne and Michael. **Bishop** Noel Willoughby is followed by the **booksellers** John Davey and Fred Hanna who join ex-model Sharon Bacon, Howard Kilroy, Ken Peare, Hilary Pratt and Don Tidey as some of the **businessmen** (and women) featured. **Canon** David Moynan and **cartoonist** Tom Mathews provide the high 'C's, a note which was well known to **conductor** Arthur Nachstern, once leader of the R.T.E. Symphony Orchestra. **Communications Consultant**, Al Byrne and **County Coroner**, Bartley Sheehan create a bit of an alphabetical gap, filled only by **general all-rounders**, Dorothy Kilroy, Dorothy Robbie, Barbara Robinson-Smyth and Margaret Thompson. Legal eagles, Maurice Abrahamson, **Judges** Ronnie Appleton, Gerard Buchanan and Hubert Wine and the Hon. Mr. **Justice** Declan Budd are followed by **Knitwear designer**, Joan Millar and **Maritime Historian**, John de Courcy Ireland. The **medics** are represented by a very experienced sextet of Geoff Chadwick, Michael Earley, Peter Gatenby, David Lane, Professor James McCormick and Niall Webb. There are a lot of 'Ps' in the pod including **photographers** Barbara Cluskey (an ex-model) and

Tom Lawlor, **physiotherapist**, Marie-Elaine Grant and R.T.E. **presenter and producer** John Quinn. Current **Presidents** who contributed are Wendy-Jane Catherwood (of the I.A.V.I.), Marie Danaswamy (of Compass and also Vice President of the National Council, Post Primary) and Sr. Stanislaus Kennedy (of Focus Ireland) and other **Professors** include Derek Briggs FRS (of Palaeontology at Bristol) and Wallace Ewart OBE (Pro Vice Chancellor/Provost at the University of Ulster). The **property** business is also represented by Roger Handy while the literary horde is completed by **publishers** (and editors) Mary Davies and Edwin Higel. Ex-**Racing Driver**, now businesswoman, Rosemary Smith speeds in here. I am not familiar with the collective noun for **Senators** but we are pleased to present Mary Henry, David Norris, Feargal Quinn and Shane Ross, all of which have numerous other interests. They are followed by **singer and songwriter**, Chris de Burgh, **solicitor**, Clodagh Kean, **sportsmen**, past and present, in Ken Haughton, Christy O'Connor Junior and John Treacy and perhaps most logically, by **T.D.**, Ruairi Quinn, Leader of the Labour Party. The **teaching** profession is well represented by the inseparable Eileen Good and Carol Porter, Niall McMonagle and Stella Mew (Principal at Rathdown). Finally, who more appropriate to have the last words than **T.V. presenter**, Gloria Hunniford and **U.N. High Commissioner**, Mary Robinson.